Poetry Explorers 2009

The East & South East England

Edited by Lisa Adlam

First published in Great Britain in 2009 by

Young**Writers**

Remus House
Coltsfoot Drive
Peterborough
PE2 9JX
Telephone: 01733 890066
Website: www.youngwriters.co.uk

All Rights Reserved
Book Design by Spencer Hart
© Copyright Contributors 2009
SB ISBN 978-1-84924-527-2

Foreword

At Young Writers our defining aim is to promote an enjoyment of reading and writing amongst children and young adults. By giving aspiring poets the opportunity to see their work in print, their love of the written word as well as confidence in their own abilities has the chance to blossom.

Our latest competition Poetry Explorers was designed to introduce primary school children to the wonders of creative expression. They were given free reign to write on any theme and in any style, thus encouraging them to use and explore a variety of different poetic forms.

We are proud to present the resulting collection of regional anthologies which are an excellent showcase of young writing talent. With such a diverse range of entries received, the selection process was difficult yet very rewarding. From comical rhymes to poignant verses, there is plenty to entertain and inspire within these pages. We hope you agree that this collection bursting with imagination is one to treasure.

Contents

Bawdsey CE(VC) Primary School, Woodbridge
Eliza Burkitt (7) 1

Birchwood Primary School, Martlesham Heath
Naomi Wilkins & Taelor Langstone (9) ... 1

Broad Oak Community Primary School, Heathfield
Ajay Archer (10) 2
Abbie Oakes (11) 2
Olivia Foskett (11) 3
Zoe Mepham (11) 3
Max Robards (10) 4
Michael King (11) 4
Charlotte Simmons (11) 5
Brandon Johnson (10) 5
Emily Turner (11) 6
Glenn Manning (11) 6
Calum Logan (10) 6
Marley Davis (11) 7
Jed Barrell (11) 7
Cameron Fyfe (11) 7
Joshua Hanks (11) 8
Elizabeth Wilsher (10) 8
Charlotte Chapman (10) 8
Joshua Rose (11) 9
Hannah Dennis (11) 9
Danielle Bates (11) 9

Charters Ancaster College, Bexhill-on-Sea
Emily Bracken (11) 10
Connie Pope (9) 11

Lucy Mercer (10) 11
Lewis Hollebon 12

Claydon Primary School, Ipswich
Katie Wright (10) 12
Rosie Bound (9) 13
Charlotte West (9) 14
Samantha Witherall (9) 15
Chloe Chandler (11) 16
Rob Borrett (10) 17
Sophie Davey (9) 17
Rebecca Clarke (11) 18
Harriet Godber (9) 19
Emma Barkell Cook (11) 19
Emily Reeder (11) 20
Emma Ibbotson (10) 20
Katie Barkell Cook (9) 21
Louisa Pannifer (10) 21

Earl Soham Primary School, Woodbridge
Lily Woodruff (8) 22
Polly Speight (10) 22
Callie Hunt (9) 23
Imogen Holland-Howes (10) 23
Klara Ashwell (9) 24
Murray Holland-Howes (8) 24
Callum Buntrock (9) 24
Jessica Giblett (9) 25

Fen Park CP School, Lowestoft
Harry Blaxell (9) 25
Callum Mager (8) 25

Ixworth Middle School, Bury St Edmunds
Georgia Walker (10) 26
James Gibson (11) 27

Emily Thomas (11) 28
Jack Martin (11) 29
Molly King (10) 30
Dani Bonnelykke (11) 31
Harvey Pearson (10) 32

Lothingland Middle School, Lound

Callum Howard (11) 32
Oliver George (11) 33
Liam French (11) 34
Pierce Mitchell & Bradley Shears (11) .. 35
Lily McKechnie (11) 36
Summer Harrowven (11) 36
Bethany Paisley (11) 37
Ebony Harvey (10) 37
Charlotte Button (11) 38
Jack Prettyman (11) 38
Ellie Rayner (11) 39
Eve Shipton (11) 39
Elliott Nichols (11) 40
Taylor Anderson (11) 40
Xene Morrison (11) 41
Adam Conolly (11) 41
Emily Gilbert (11) 42
Lily Adjemian (10) & Jorden Lewis (11) 42
Tom Evans (10) 43
Harrison Broadfoot (11) 43
Bryony Rogers (10) 44
Stacey Lambert (11) 44
Victoria Stone (11) 45
Katie Felgate (11) 45
William Hilton (11) 46
Charlie Church (11) 46
Charlie Cassidy (11) 47
Ruby Oldman (11) 47
Regwaan Choudhury (11) 48
Kate Loveday (11) 48
Hannah Illingsworth (11) 48
Liam Walpole & Liam Clews (11) 49
Ewen Keleher (11) 49
Rebecca Reynolds (10) 49
Kirstie Leech (11) 50
Ianthe Harvey (11) 50

Ashleigh Broughton (11) 50
Olivia Seago (11) 51

Marshlands CP School, Hailsham

Lewis Parsons (10) 51
Chloe Fudger (10) 52
Tyler Rigglesford (9) 53
Maryann Stonestreet (9) 53
Chloe Breeds (11) 54
Connor McLaughlan (10) 54
Connor Townsend (9) 55
Joseph Hutchinson (10) 55
Cherelle McLaughlan (9) 56
Jason Rogers (10) 56
Liam Smith (9) 56
Charlie Williams (9) 57

Rocks Park Primary School, Uckfield

Shannon Limberger (8) 57
James Batstone (11) 58
Kieran Batstone (8) 59
Max Goodwin (9) 60
Harry Limberger (8) 61
Callum Fuller-Iles (11) 62
Christian Martin (9) 63
Karl Milton (11) 63
Syimyk Kyshtoobaev (9) 64
Benjamin Ricketts (9) 65
Jessica Armstrong (8) 66
Lauren Vane (8) 67
Declan Bromfield (10) 67
Megan Miles (9) 68
Olivia Baldwin (9) 69
Luke Oakley (9) 70
Connie Swaysland-Neal (11) 70
Hannah Baker (9) 71
Chloe Marriott (9) 72
Ben French (8) 73
Millie Hague (9) 74
Fraser Munn (8) 75
Rachelle Griffith (11) 75
Elizabeth Trigwell (9) 76
Georgia Lock (11) 76

Katie Nettleton (8)	77
James Munn (11)	77
Stephen Williams (11)	78
Harrison Terry (10)	78
Ellie Smith (11)	79
Matthew Pilcher (10)	79
Alexandra Lane (10)	80
Zaveri Shah-Smith (8)	81
Sadie Dix (9)	82
Jack Foster (11)	83
Bethany Maw (10)	83
Abigail Hale (11)	84
Aston Baden (9)	84
Claire Robinson (9)	85
Charley Baker (11)	85
Rees Rider (9)	86

SS Peter & Paul CE Primary School, Bexhill-on-Sea

Jake Reader (11)	86
May Drawbridge (11)	87
Alexander Clark (11)	87
Ben Saunders (11)	88
Samuel Bayliss (11)	88
Rowena Habadah (11)	89
Fiona Rumary (11)	89
Bethany Claridge (11)	90
Natasha Wilding De Miranda (11)	90
Joshua Kildea (11)	91
Fleur Lawrie (10)	91
Amber Cruttenden (11)	92
Liam McGarry (11)	92
Megan Wilson (11)	93
Joshua Ruane (11)	93
Joe Mowbray (10)	94
Beth Jeffery (11)	94
Charlotte Durtnall (11)	95
Samuel May (11)	95
Callum Green (11)	96
Eloise Jeffery (11)	96
Lucy Tucknott (11)	97
Emma Rushbrooke (11)	97
Simon Richardson (10)	97

Ben Smith (10)	98
Amy Izzard (11)	98
Max Woolfrey (11)	98
Linley Ross (11)	99
Ben Flenley (11)	99
Maartje Deeprose (11)	99
Simon Tomlinson (11)	100
Tom Eden (11)	100
Amber Stubbs (10)	100
Adele Vincent (11)	101
Reece Beard (11)	101
Emily Hobbs (10)	101
Reilly McDonnell (11)	102
George Robinson (11)	102
Louis Wicks (10)	102
Archie Whittaker (11)	102
Kieran Inglis (11)	103

St Helen's CP School, Ipswich

Shelby Haynes (10)	103
Maia Shouksmith (8)	103
Hafizur Hussain Ullah (10)	104
Lee Thorpe (11)	104
Katy Jane Forrester (11)	105
Charlie-Louise Parker (9)	105
Charlie Woodage (10)	106
Mohammed Imran (8)	106
Jack Iddon (11)	106
Ines Bowman-Boyles (7)	107
Anushka Ghiya (8)	107
Broghan Ellis (8)	107
Perran Hugo King (7)	108
Katherine Hurley (10)	108
Felix Todd (10)	109
Naia Brown-Powell (9)	110
Hannah Noble (7)	110
Louisa Pisaturo (8)	111
Rhiannon Lugo (9)	111
Alima Aktar (11)	112
Rishawn Mohamed (8)	112
Daisy Bissett (9)	113
Dora Densham Bond (9)	113
Jordan Romero (11)	114

Natasha Smith (9)	114
Chloe Hickman (9)	115
Willow Kirkby (11)	115
Will Disney (11)	116
Liam Roberts (9)	116
Kassandra Hamm (9)	117
Bailey Robinson (9)	117
Harry Holian (11)	118
Chloe Parkin (9)	118
Charlotte Simms (9)	118
Andrew Chenery (10)	119
Ellen Lear (10)	119
Shumie Akhtar (11)	119
Nasim Miah (9)	120
Samuel Clarke (11)	120
Halima Sultana (9)	120
Kirsty Simms (9)	121
William Stewart (9)	121
Afjal Miah (9)	121
Farjana Aktar (9)	122
Baker Kagimu (9)	122
Priyanka Bikkannavar (9)	122
Esther Noble (9)	123
Samuel Clarkson (9)	123
Jack Butler Pearson (9)	123
Sam Jones (9)	124
Arifha Aktar (9)	124
Rebecca Lewis (9)	124
Kean Fry (11)	125
Moya-Alice Bowman (11)	125
John Monge (9)	125
Nadir Islam (10)	126
Lindsey Page-Mason (9)	126
Sophie Turner (10)	126
Molly Gooding (9)	127
Jacob Kirkby (8)	127
Clare Parker (10)	127
Amy Goodger (9)	128
Sian Chapman (8)	128
Faimah Sultana (7)	128
Musomie Aktar (8)	129
Owen Miller (10)	129
Chloe Watson-Boyle (9)	129

St John's CE (VA) Primary School, Ipswich

Eleanor Hitchings (9)	130
Amelia Calderhead (10)	131
Oliver Page (9)	132
Ryan O'Shea (9)	133
Charlotte Housego (9)	134
Huda Abd (10)	135
Joshua Moore (10)	135
Harriet Hughes (10)	136
Bethany Kenward (10)	137
Thomas Floodgate (10)	137
Kezia Davey (10)	138

St Mary Magdalene's RC Primary School, Bexhill-on-Sea

Abbie Jones (11)	138
Ellie Stebbing (11)	139
Jessie Sheppard (11)	140
Lois Tucker (11)	141
Amelia Catherine Markfort (11)	142
Isaac Klugman (8)	142
Lauren Mary Louise Creasey (10)	143
Yasmin Davis (10)	143
Jessica Cumming-Bart (11)	144
Miriam Calis (10)	144
Mollie Docksey (9)	145
Annabel Selvadurai (9)	145
Mickey Cross (8)	146
John Rey Ruiz (11)	146
Georgina May Pepper (11)	147
Chloe Leigh Fox (11)	147
Hassan Takun (11)	148
Niall MacDonald (11)	148
Olivia Mackrell (11)	149
Sophie Barret & Holly Wicks (10)	149
Alice Creasey (8)	150
Ciaran Gaymer (10)	150
Katie Wilson (11)	151
Andrew Creasy (10)	151
Lauren Leigh Henson (11)	152
Carys Rebecca Williams (10)	152

Jordan Billany (11) 153
Joe Lissamore (8) 153
Olivia Murphy (10) 153
Karina Barton-Monk (8) 154
Olivia West (9) 154
Renie Vince (10) 154
Samuel Boreham (8) 155
Charlie Bonner (8) 155

Sacred Heart School, Wadhurst

Chiara Vidal (8) 155
Elizabeth Trippett (9) 156
Oliver Taylor (8) 157
Louis Griffiths (8) 157
Eleanor Knight (7) 158
Rebecca Lond (7) 158
Harry Thatcher (7) 159
Theo Griffiths (8) 159
Ben Sanday (8) 160
Michael Ghose (8) 160
Eloise Langdon (8) 161

South Wootton First School, Kings Lynn

Rhys Brown (8) 161
Megan Savage (8) 162
Adam White (8) 162
Eden Daniell (8) 163
Aimée Colman (8) 163
Aimee Tivey (8) 164
Sefton Henry Shillingford (8) 164
Carla Sayer (8) 164
Benita Bausbacher (8) 165

The Norman CE Primary School, Northwold

Kirstie Windsor (9) 165
Harry Cater (8) 165
Ella Wortley (8) 166
Abigail Gostling (9) 166
Alice Ireland (7) 167
Olivia Rae (8) 167
Hannah Bradford (8) 167

Euan Bradford (8) 168
Amber Harris (10) 168
Kya Raven (9) 168
Hannah Muir (10) 169

The Poems

The Heavy Elephant

On the savannah I tread,
I have *big* ears upon my head!
I rule the grasslands day by day,
I just wish those pesky flies would go away!
I will nuzzle you if you are a friend,
And gently to your wounds I will tend.
Sometimes when a truck roars round the bend,
My group of wives I loyally defend.

Eliza Burkitt (7)
Bawdsey CE(VC) Primary School, Woodbridge

Standing In My School In Winter

Standing in my school in winter I can see
The fluffy snow falling like candy,
Crisp cover of cotton candy snow that crunches underfoot,
Snowflakes trembling on my shoulder,
That's what I see

Standing in my school in winter I can hear
The wicked wind whistling away in the distance
Laughter of the children playing
Snowballs crashing against the wall
That's what I hear

Standing in my school in winter I can feel
The cold crisp biting at my skin
The spikes of ice prickling my feet
The snow dropping dramatically on my face
That's what I feel

Standing in my school in winter I can smell
Wet wellie boots warming up on the radiator
Floppy gloves like fish that cannot be warmed
Hot chocolate wafting up my nose
That's what I can smell.

Naomi Wilkins & Taelor Langstone (9)
Birchwood Primary School, Martlesham Heath

Mysterious Kennings

It's a . . .

Flower sticker
Petal picker
Stripy seeker
House peeker
Honey maker
Pollen taker
Flying buzzer
Furry fuzzer
Creepy creature
Stinging feature
Hive builder
Flower fielder.

What is my insect?

Ajay Archer (10)
Broad Oak Community Primary School, Heathfield

Abbie's Kennings

It's a . . .
Slow mover
Slimy slider
Trail leaver
Leaf eater
Garden killer
Home remover
Shell liver
Horn expander
Dull colour
Heavy sleeper
It's a . . .

Snail.

Abbie Oakes (11)
Broad Oak Community Primary School, Heathfield

The Dragonfly

It is a . . .

Quick darter,
Fast flyer,
Water skimmer,
Reed climber,
Breeze rider,
Skilled hider,
Sight catcher,
Mind transfixer,
Attention drawer,
Soft buzzer . . .

It's a dragonfly!

Olivia Foskett (11)
Broad Oak Community Primary School, Heathfield

Zoe's Kennings

It's a . . .

Smooth glider
Colourful flyer
Wing flapper
Sun lover
Flower attractor
Leaf eater
Nectar dipper
Wild dancer

My insect is a
Butterfly.

Zoe Mepham (11)
Broad Oak Community Primary School, Heathfield

Max's Kennings

It's a:
Leaf chewer,
Tree climber,
Slow mover,
Many legger,
Hairy backer,
Cocoon spinner,
Bird's dinner.

It's a . . .
Caterpillar.

Max Robards (10)
Broad Oak Community Primary School, Heathfield

Michael's Kennings Poem

It's a . . .
Fast flyer,
Blue sparkler,
Prancing dancer,
Water skimmer,
Quiet buzzer,
Quick darter,
Eye catcher,
So it must be a . . .
Dragonfly.

Michael King (11)
Broad Oak Community Primary School, Heathfield

It Is . . .

It's a . . .
Smooth mover,
Dazzling dancer,
Bright colour,
Flower wanderer,
Fast flyer,
Eye catcher,
Pretty whisperer,
It is a . . .
Butterfly.

Charlotte Simmons (11)
Broad Oak Community Primary School, Heathfield

Brandon's Kennings

It's a . . .
Super zoomer
Flower bloomer
Wasp's neighbour
Lots of labour
Nectar collector
Hive protector
Brilliant stinger
Dies after.
It's a bee.

Brandon Johnson (10)
Broad Oak Community Primary School, Heathfield

Emily's Kennings

It is a . . .

Colourful flyer
Attention drawer
Swift mover
Smooth glider
Leaf eater
Wild dancer

The insect is a . . .
Butterfly.

Emily Turner (11)
Broad Oak Community Primary School, Heathfield

Glenn's Kennings

It's an . . .
Aphid eater
Ant beater
Swift swooper
Bright spotter
Poison maker
Fast flyer
What am I?

Ladybird.

Glenn Manning (11)
Broad Oak Community Primary School, Heathfield

Ant - Haiku

Black, shining body
Food carrier for the tribe
Always marching home.

Calum Logan (10)
Broad Oak Community Primary School, Heathfield

Marley's Kennings

It's a . . .

Silk spinner
Fast runner
Moth killer
Bug eater
Creepy crawler
Finger biter.

It's a spider.

Marley Davis (11)
Broad Oak Community Primary School, Heathfield

Spider

It's a . . .

Web spinner
Bug beater
Fast runner
Creepy crawler
Moth eater
Eight walker
It's a spider.

Jed Barrell (11)
Broad Oak Community Primary School, Heathfield

It's A . . .

Home keeper
Slow mover
Armoured trooper
Leaf muncher
Plant killer
Bird's dinner

What am I?

Cameron Fyfe (11)
Broad Oak Community Primary School, Heathfield

Scorpion Poem

S cary little creature
C urved, spiky tail
O rangey-tinged colour
R obot-looking bug
P est when you eat
I nsect, no it's not!
O h no, even claws!
N o! It's a scorpion!

Joshua Hanks (11)
Broad Oak Community Primary School, Heathfield

Dragonfly

Wings sparkling in the sunlight like a sweet wrapper.
It hovers over a nearby pond,
As it weaves through the reeds that are like trees,
Towering above it.
So delicate you would not dare handle it.
This is a dragonfly,
Flying past my window,
In the summer sunlight.

Elizabeth Wilsher (10)
Broad Oak Community Primary School, Heathfield

The Dragonfly

The dragonfly
Delicate wings so smooth and silky
Eyes like shining crystals
Glowing in the bright sunlight
The dragonfly opens its wings
Skims the deep blue waters
Shining from high to low
That's the dragonfly.

Charlotte Chapman (10)
Broad Oak Community Primary School, Heathfield

A Butterfly

A butterfly flies so sweet
It glitters in the sunlight
And it makes it look so neat
With its wingspan and its pretty pattern
It's so beautiful.
It gleams as it flies
A golden surprise.

Joshua Rose (11)
Broad Oak Community Primary School, Heathfield

The Dragonfly

A dragonfly is a wonderful insect
That shimmers in the sun
And has a lovely reflection in the pond
In your back garden.
It flies by your eye
And you can tell the dragonfly
Has visited your back garden and you.

Hannah Dennis (11)
Broad Oak Community Primary School, Heathfield

Danielle's Kennings

Fast flyer
Loud buzzer
Bright colour
Might sting
It's a . . .
Wasp.

Danielle Bates (11)
Broad Oak Community Primary School, Heathfield

The Diary

I sit on a tall, dark shelf,
Lined, blank pages, desperate to be filled.
She picks me up, today bursting with happiness,
She embroiders my white page with flowers and hearts,
Writing about her day.
I am her forever friend,
We get on well and never argue.
I am there for her when she is lonely
And she explains all her troubles.
Together we think them out.
I keep every secret, every teardrop, every thought
Hidden away under lock and key.
She comes in angry and upset.
I am close to her and she throws me across the room.
I lie in a corner.
Will I ever know what happened today?
Will she remember me and fill me in?
April the ninth, April the ninth.
She comes over sobbing,
Picks me up, stroking down my new creases.
She unlocks me and I learn her sadness.
I forgive her for throwing me for she is so unhappy.
After writing, her tears are gone,
She knows what to do.
She smiles at me. I am important to her.
Her best friend.

Emily Bracken (11)
Charters Ancaster College, Bexhill-on-Sea

The Magic Door

I stepped through the magic door and saw
A rag doll, old and antique, smiling at me.

I wandered through the magic door and saw
A fire-breathing dragon drinking pineapple juice.

I ran through the magic door and saw
A crystal rainbow gleaming over a deep lake.

I was pushed through the magic door and saw
A dark, cloudy night drifting into silence.

I skipped through the magic door and saw
A cereal box chatting and singing.

I walked through the magic door and saw
Dolphins leaping, jumping and diving through the sun.

Connie Pope (9)
Charters Ancaster College, Bexhill-on-Sea

Horses

Hay for breakfast,
Hay for dinner,
A black and white blur in a mirror.
They race through the fields,
Gracefully moving
In the silent lavender air.
Their shiny hooves
Flash with a golden streak,
Brittle tails flick and flop.
Smooth silken coats
Shining in the moonlight.

Lucy Mercer (10)
Charters Ancaster College, Bexhill-on-Sea

Water

Tears drip tensely and crash in shallow puddles
Pipes burst suddenly and get in great muddles
Ducks swim slowly in the deep blue lake
And a hosepipe hisses like a venomous snake.

Rivers gush quickly down to the sea
And saucepans drizzle loudly cooking the tea
Clouds thunder viciously and control great lightning
While storms rumble fiercely getting so frightening.

Lewis Hollebon
Charters Ancaster College, Bexhill-on-Sea

My Dog, Elsa

My dog, Elsa,
She's soon to be three,
She's a beautiful girl,
But no pedigree.

My dog, Elsa,
She's called a springerdor,
Not a complete spaniel,
She's half a Labrador.

My dog, Elsa,
She loves her walks,
She wags her tail
And almost talks.

My dog, Elsa,
She loves to play,
She brings her football
To me every day.

We are best of friends,
Elsa and me,
Like we will always be!

Katie Wright (10)
Claydon Primary School, Ipswich

Poetry Explorers 2009 - The East & South East England

My Best Friend

At five days old I see my new friend,
Somehow I know I'll be with her to the end.
At first I cannot run and play
But I know I'm going to love her in every way.

As I begin to crawl and walk
I even share her bed to read and talk.
Does she understand me? I'm not sure
But these special times I simply adore.

So now I'm four I can walk a long way,
It's off to the river for a run and a play.
She launches herself in and swims like a fish,
Why can't I do that? I just watch and wish.

Now it's off in the Land Rover to a camping site,
We put up the tent in the sunny daylight.
Then it's time for bed with the stars so bright
But I know she'll protect me right through the night.

To my birthday parties friends and family come
She welcomes them, every single one.
Games in the garden and a birthday tea
At the end of the day she is still there for me.

Home from school she is always there
I give her a hug and show her I care.
I teach her all sorts of funny tricks
And that was when I was only six.

The picnics on the beach, on the sand we run
Oh, the adventures we had were such fun.
Dashing and splashing through the foamy sea
Running and chasing, she can't catch me.

So *she* is Pebbles, the best dog there ever could be
Me and her are best friends you see.
Always and forever you know
But sadly the time has come to say cheerio.

Rosie Bound (9)
Claydon Primary School, Ipswich

Dogs

I went to buy my dog
Everyone laughed
Because they said he looked like a frog

I didn't care
Everyone looked at me
Because he looked a bit bare

On the way home, he was sick
Ahhhh! It stunk!
At least it was only a bit

When we got in
He loved it
Especially the bin

We went to bed
He found a pencil
He liked the lead

The next day
We went to a farm
He found a stack of hay

When we went for a walk
He pulled and pulled
Then I realised that he could talk

We went to the park
Woof, woof
He barked

We got home
I had to go to work
Ahh! He was alone.

Charlotte West (9)
Claydon Primary School, Ipswich

A Fairy From San Francisco

A fairy from San Francisco
Went to a disco
But didn't know how to dance.

A pixie from the South Pole
Went to bowl
But the ball was too heavy.

An elf from Ecuador
Became a matador
But was scared of the bull.

A mermaid from Madagascar
Went to Alaska
But was tired halfway through.

A troll from Turkey
Went somewhere murky
But ran away screaming like a girl.

An alien from the Constellation Aquarius
Wanted to be the scariest
But was just too cute.

A witch from the west
Wanted to have a test
But did not have all the answers.

A girl from the UK
Decided to fly away
And that was me!

Bye!

Samantha Witherall (9)
Claydon Primary School, Ipswich

The Dragon

The dragon is haunting,
Ghostly and taunting.
His scales glittering gold,
Sparkling in the moonlight,
He will put up a great fight
For all the children fear,
One day,
Just one day,
He'll get you!

The dragon is slick
And could kill in a tick.
His eyes are black spheres,
Everybody fears,
One day,
Just one day,
He'll get you!

The dragon is a liar,
His breath is on fire,
Never dare
To enter his dark lair,
To the villages he brings tears,
Whenever he leers near,
All people fear,
One day,
Just one day,
He'll get you.

Chloe Chandler (11)
Claydon Primary School, Ipswich

The Circus

We arrive at the big top,
And show our tickets at the door.
We go and find our seats,
Then put our belongings on the floor.
The ringmaster enters,
Who introduces all the acts,
First up it's some elephants
With people on their backs!
Next it is some monkeys
Doing amazing trapeze tricks
And a boy lying on the floor,
Juggling burning sticks.
Guess what, a clown enters,
Throwing a custard tart,
Then it is the strong man,
(That's my favourite part).
It's time to leave the circus now,
We walk into the night,
We drive back home, I get into bed
And I am out like a light.

Rob Borrett (10)
Claydon Primary School, Ipswich

My School

My school is the best
Of them all in the west
When the teachers rest
We don't make a lot of mess
So teachers carry on doing your best
And we will always do our test!

Sophie Davey (9)
Claydon Primary School, Ipswich

Puffins

Puffins
Need help,
Cute or dead,
Their beautiful yellow beaks
Need your help to survive,
This could be your last chance,
So please save them, now or never,
They are animals but they have feelings too,
So stop eating them for breakfast, lunch and dinner,
They may not be endangered right now, but just wait,
Puffins will be endangered then extinct, you will see,
We do not want to say goodbye forever,
So stop and think about the puffins,
The poor, defenceless animals need you,
Don't wait until they're gone
To love the puffins,
Food or beauty,
Please help
Puffins.

Rebecca Clarke (11)
Claydon Primary School, Ipswich

The Woods

The sun glistened
Through the trees,
While the wind whistled
In the air.

At night in the woods
It gets very dark,
If you're lucky you might
See a badger or a hedgehog.

In autumn, crispy leaves
Start to fall to the ground,
When you walk over them
They make a loud crunching sound.

There are lots of
Different types of trees in the woods,
The forests are exciting and fun
To explore and build dens in.

Harriet Godber (9)
Claydon Primary School, Ipswich

Fragile World

Imagine our world
A quarter of its size,
Imagine our world
With no blue skies,
Imagine our world
Where most animals are dead,
Imagine our world
When we're hardly fed,
Imagine our world
Full of misery and sadness,
Think of our world now
And save it from this madness!

Emma Barkell Cook (11)
Claydon Primary School, Ipswich

A Stream From The Heart

A flowing stream of love that never ends,
Never will it stop looking for a friend.
The heart that has no muscle for support,
That's why it flows downhill and feels distraught.

In any crazy condition,
It'll make a spell like a magician,
To keep strong and continue the search!

Like its seeking love,
Sent from the heavens above,
If failing the quest
And not passing their test,
It evaporates and turns into rain,
Starting the search all over again!

Emily Reeder (11)
Claydon Primary School, Ipswich

Daffodils

They start off as bulbs
That are planted underground,
The rain visits again
And the sun comes out.
The daffodils grow,
First the stem and leaves,
Then the bud.
At long last it is the flower I can see.
They last for a while,
But then they start to droop.
Poor little daffodils,
See you again soon!

Emma Ibbotson (10)
Claydon Primary School, Ipswich

My Chickens

I love my chickens so very much,
My dad and I made the hutch.
They do not fly very high,
But in the sun they like to lie.
With fluffy bottoms they waddle about,
'Off my flowers!' you hear Mum shout.
They spend all day pecking for food,
Being ignored puts them in a bad mood.
When eggs are laid we shout hooray,
Eggs are great to eat or to give away.
On their perches they sleep,
Chickens are great to keep.

Katie Barkell Cook (9)
Claydon Primary School, Ipswich

The Ruler Of The Night

The ruler of the night
Glides through the sky,
Old, wide, wise eyes shimmer,
Brighter than amber,
Piercing the dark night.

Swooping down with all his might,
Talons ready to seize and squeeze,
Beak as sharp as a knife,
Feathers ruffled,
Ready for a fight.

Who . . . who . . . who . . .?

Louisa Pannifer (10)
Claydon Primary School, Ipswich

Anger

Anger is red
Anger is blue
You stamp your feet
You're getting in a stew
You want to fight
You want to win
You're getting angry and you won't give in
You run around
And shout and scream
You need to let off some steam
Anger is red
Anger is blue
Anger doesn't suit you.

Lily Woodruff (8)
Earl Soham Primary School, Woodbridge

Anger

Anger makes me feel so cross
Anger shows me who is boss
I shake my fist and stamp my feet
It makes me jump up from my seat
Grumpy is not quite the same
It makes me feel that I'm to blame
I kick the wall
And bang my head
And throw myself down on my bed
Smiles make me feel so good
Smiles make me eat my pud
I wave my arms and jump up high
It makes me feel I'm in the sky.

Polly Speight (10)
Earl Soham Primary School, Woodbridge

Anger

When I am angry, I blow my top,
Nothing can stop me having a strop.
When I am calm, I am as good as gold,
Nothing can stop me being so bold.

When God is angry, He makes a light,
When I'm trying to sleep at night.
He bangs on his drums as loud as can be,
To make me believe He can see.

So when I am angry, I promise to be,
As good as I can so God can see.
God is up there in the sky,
Making sure I always try.

Callie Hunt (9)
Earl Soham Primary School, Woodbridge

Anger

Anger is pointy and sharp, like lightning
It peers out of the fog for someone to snap at
As if it was a big, green crocodile.

It explodes in your body
Like a great big, erupting volcano,
With red-hot lava pouring out.

Crackle,
Bubble,
Spit.

But now I look back on it,
I wonder how it ever even started.

Imogen Holland-Howes (10)
Earl Soham Primary School, Woodbridge

Anger

Anger feels like a bad dream
With monsters running after me.

Anger feels like a sea of blood
And I'm afraid of drowning.

Anger feels like lightning flashing through the sky,
When it's finally over, I often wonder why.

Klara Ashwell (9)
Earl Soham Primary School, Woodbridge

Guilt

Guilt is white, like a dragon's tooth
Guilt tastes like water going down the wrong tube
Guilt smells like overcooked bacon
Guilt looks like a box you've been shut in
Guilt sounds like men calling for help
Guilt feels like someone punching you in the stomach.

Murray Holland-Howes (8)
Earl Soham Primary School, Woodbridge

Anger

Anger is red, like sunburnt faces
It smells like a volcano
It sounds like a thunderstorm
It looks like my mum
It feels like a burning hand.

Callum Buntrock (9)
Earl Soham Primary School, Woodbridge

Anger

Anger is a frantic wasp trapped in a tiny pot,
Anger is a burning finger stuck on something hot,
Anger is a thunderstorm brewing in a blackened sky,
Anger builds and anger bursts, but soon it passes by.

Jessica Giblett (9)
Earl Soham Primary School, Woodbridge

The Cheetah

The cheetah proudly ploughed through the grass
Silently catching its prey
Running quickly through the forest
All through the day

As he lunges to his prey, diving,
Vaulting, catapulting,
This is for real, not just play

The cheetah, the fastest animal alive
Kills not for fun, but to survive
Escape from a cheetah, what animal can?
But, can the cheetah escape from Man?

Harry Blaxell (9)
Fen Park CP School, Lowestoft

The Rampage

The elephants are off, so you'd better run,
They won't stop until you give them a bun.
They're gonna break everything in their path,
Cover your ears because they're gonna *laugh*.
You'd better jump and you'd better run,
They're gonna chase and they're gonna have fun!

Callum Mager (8)
Fen Park CP School, Lowestoft

The Honeybee

The honeybee
Is disappearing quickly,
But without them
Life has no gem,
Without the honeybee . . .

Our world would be flowerless
We will be powerless;
As these bees
Pollinate flowers from gardens
To shopping sprees.
No honey,
No money
For the beekeepers,
But they'll be weepers
Without the honeybee . . .

However,
We won't live forever,
As without pollination,
We will have no vegetation.
The food chains
Shall become grains,
Without the honeybee . . .

Nothing would live,
The world like a sieve,
Without the honeybee,
Trust me,
Without the honeybee . . .

Georgia Walker (10)
Ixworth Middle School, Bury St Edmunds

A Dream

One night I started dreaming
About clouds and fluffy sheep,
When suddenly it happened,
While I was asleep.

It was not death,
Nor was it flying pigs,
It wasn't my English teacher
Changing all her wigs.

It wasn't a giraffe
Making stew,
It wasn't a tortoise
On the loo.

It was something terrible,
Something I feared,
Worse than Katy Perry
With a curly beard.

My trousers ripped at school,
The elastic didn't bend,
Now I'm not so jig and jazz,
And all with the new trend.

Ahh! What's this?
A giant light beam.
I woke up,
Phew! It was all just a dream.

James Gibson (11)
Ixworth Middle School, Bury St Edmunds

My First Day Of School

I got up out of bed,
Ready for my first day of school,
Things running through my head,
Thinking how uncool!

I went to get dressed,
Oh man, what to wear?
What if I do a test?
Do I really care?

I really didn't want to eat,
Maybe an egg or a piece of toast.
This definitely wasn't a treat,
I'd be embarrassed the most!

I walked out the door,
What if I forgot something?
This feels like a chore,
Do the school like to sing?

I get to school,
Everyone stares at me,
I think the school have a pool,
I can't swim you see!

I think it's time,
I need to show myself,
I am a teacher,
Not ready for the first day!

Emily Thomas (11)
Ixworth Middle School, Bury St Edmunds

Alone, All Alone

On a dark, cold night
By the battered street light
Flickering so bright,
All alone, no one with him,
Cold and damp,
His tongue ripped off,
Mouth on the ground,
Soul flattened
Against the wall,
The tabby cat purrs,
Settles by him,
The lights go out,
The moon is dim,
So I ask you one thing,
So please hear me out,
I will tell you once,
I won't scream or shout,
That is,
Don't forget your lonely old shoe,
Because it's at the corner,
Waiting for you!

Jack Martin (11)
Ixworth Middle School, Bury St Edmunds

Animals

Cats and kittens streaking across the floor
Faster than a car on a motorway,
Tiger cubs pounding on their mums
As if they were on a springy trampoline.

Giraffes striding around, reaching up
As they try to grab some leaves to gobble up,
Elephants plodding around
Like someone hitting drums; 1, 2; 1, 2.

Monkeys squeaking, swinging on branches
Like little kids on playground swings,
Hippos lazing in the sun
Using the mud as if it was a deckchair.

Cows grazing on the grass,
Snaffling up almost all the grass.
Puppies barking so loud,
It sounds like they are barking through a loudspeaker.

Mice squeaking searching for cheese
Like they were on a treasure hunt.

Molly King (10)
Ixworth Middle School, Bury St Edmunds

Our Head Teacher

Our head teacher is a bit of a nutter
Because she slipped on some butter.
She went to the doctor to look at her head
Even though she fell out of her bed.
She had a big bruise
That started to ooze
'Cause she slipped on some butter.

Our head teacher has recovered now
Even though she broke her crown.
We all think she is bonkers
'Cause she's going on about conkers.
Now I am going home
I want to go to the dome.
It has been an exciting day
So now we will all go out and play, yay!

Our head teacher is a bit of a nutter
'Cause she slipped on some butter!

Dani Bonnelykke (11)
Ixworth Middle School, Bury St Edmunds

My Family

My little sis
Wants a kiss

My little bro
Wants to play with a crow

My little cousin
Likes the sound of bees buzzin'

My big dad
Is so mad

My clever mum
Is never dumb

I am good anyway
So bow down to me today!

Harvey Pearson (10)
Ixworth Middle School, Bury St Edmunds

False Alarm

Sirens blaring out,
Running to a false alarm.
Rushing to and fro,
Firemen, paramedics,
Children playing with a phone.

Wasting people's time,
Only call when you need them!
Someone could need help.
They have no idea that you
Don't really need them at all.

Please don't call them out
If you just want to have fun,
This isn't just some fun.
Play something else,
Like skipping, man hunt or exercise.

Callum Howard (11)
Lothingland Middle School, Lound

Darkness

Slowly, slowly the darkness creeps
Along the land as the people sleep,
Behold, behold the moon's alight,
Following the darkness so bright, so bright.

During the day the people say,
The moon has gone, it's gone away,
The darkness hiding in the sky,
Above the clouds so high, so high.

Silently, silently like a snake,
The darkness comes for the white moon's sake,
As every bird moves swiftly by,
The trees wave quietly to the changing sky.

Ticking, ticking, the time just flies,
As the darkness looks with its silver eyes,
Oh, dogs and wolves will howl and howl,
As misty souls will scowl and scowl.

Now evening's gone and midnight waits,
Those stars still glitter like shining plates,
And on those stars of silvery gold,
The planets wave to the land of old.

Yesterday has been left behind
And darkness has come to play with my mind.
Animals play with darkness' child,
As the weather stays so mild, so mild.

Darkness has gone now, it's far away,
I'm just so glad it's not here to stay.
The bright, bright sun is smiling at me,
Hovering over the deep blue sea.

Oliver George (11)
Lothingland Middle School, Lound

Footballer

Football, football
What can you do?
Well, I'll show you
What I can do.

Step-overs
Drag backs
Curls
And kicks

Shooting
Scoring
Passing
And flicks.

Player, player
What can you do?
Well, I'll show you
What I can do.

High kicks
Dink flicks
Tricks
And overhead kicks

Dribbling
Defending
Goal saving
And perfect nicks.

Liam French (11)
Lothingland Middle School, Lound

The Magic Box
(Based on 'Magic Box' by Kit Wright)

I will put in the box . . .
The rarest dragon egg from the Middle Ages,
The farthest galaxy away from our Earth,
A pot of gold from the end of the rainbow.

I will put in the box . . .
A person made of jelly,
The scale from the shiniest tropical fish,
The last woolly mammoth from the Ice Age.

I will put in the box . . .
The rain that tastes like apple juice,
The last cackle from my grandma,
The new sun each day.

I will put in the box . . .
A space shuttle soaring from Jupiter,
An elf wearing a tutu
And a ballerina wearing elfin shoes.

My box is fashioned from the oldest oak tree
And the sun's last flame.
The hinges are created from the largest alligator's jaws.

I shall venture in my box
To the bottom of the ocean
To find the lost city of Atlantis
Whilst riding on a giant squid.

Pierce Mitchell & Bradley Shears (11)
Lothingland Middle School, Lound

The Magic Box
(Based on 'Magic Box' by Kit Wright)

I will put in my box . . .
The song of a tropical bird,
A lock of hair from a leprechaun,
The first ever diamond in the world.

I will put in my box . . .
The shine of a star on a summer night,
A dark feather from a dodo,
The coolness of a cucumber.

I will put in my box . . .
A penny from a Parisian's pocket,
The soft fire of a phoenix feather,
The razzle-dazzle of a rainbow.

I will put in my box . . .
The cry of a dying elephant,
The laughter of a hyena,
The shriek of a hunting eagle.

My box is fashioned from the finest gold,
With sparkles on the lid and whispers in the corners.
Its hinges are shiny seashells from the shores of Scotland.

In my box I will soar through the fluffiest of clouds,
Swim through the deepest ocean
And run the longest track within a second.

Lily McKechnie (11)
Lothingland Middle School, Lound

Frogs - Tanka

Nice green animals,
French people come to eat them,
Hiding from the French,
Quick, hide, they are now coming,
We don't want to go, so hide.

Summer Harrowven (11)
Lothingland Middle School, Lound

Something

As wet as a fish
As woolly as a sheep
As cold as a penguin
As happy as a hyena

As stripy as a zebra
As blind as a bat
As fast as a cheetah
As high as a bird

As cute as a kitten
As small as a mouse
As fierce as a lion
As slow as a snail

As bouncy as a bunny
As furry as a dog
As crazy as a monkey
As buzzy as a bee

I don't know
If it's gonna be in snow
Or if it's gonna show
Cos it doesn't even know
What it is!

Bethany Paisley (11)
Lothingland Middle School, Lound

Secrets

S *hhh*, don't tell
E ven if it is tempting
C lose to telling
R andom notes I'll tell
E asy writing down notes
T he most important speech
S *hhh*, don't say a word.

Ebony Harvey (10)
Lothingland Middle School, Lound

Woolly Fiend

A slow walker
A grass muncher
A string snapper
A plant luncher

A night hater
A breeze liker
A noise fearer
A field hiker

A straw breaker
A fuss seeker
A low warbler
A wet bleaker

A branch ripper
A warm jumper
A food spiller
A fat flumper . . .

My sheep.

Charlotte Button (11)
Lothingland Middle School, Lound

Soldier

S olid as a diamond
O ut of danger
L ike a tiger creeping up on its prey
D ie with pride
I ndian enemy closing in
E erie noises
R attling guns

D rowning in sweat and tears
I n enemy territory
E erie silence
S hot in an instant.

Jack Prettyman (11)
Lothingland Middle School, Lound

Hairbrush

'Use me! Use me!' she screams,
demanding me to get out of bed and pick her up.
She blinks her long, curvy eyelashes in the sunlight
And grins as she sits on the window sill.
She struts poshly as she reaches my hair,
Showing off.
She thinks she is so great.
As I use her, she clings to my hair
And won't let go of the tangled strands.
I shriek, 'Ow, ow! You're hurting!'
But she just ignores me.
She thinks she's smart,
She thinks she's clever,
But actually, she just hurts.
She's as prickly as a hedgehog.
Thankfully, it gets all the knots out,
But the dreadful thing is,
It happens all again tomorrow morning.

Ellie Rayner (11)
Lothingland Middle School, Lound

Memory Dash

The race is about to begin,
With my childhood memories versus my hopes and dreams,
Followed by my holiday thoughts versus my Year 5 memory teams.
The whistle blows and off they go as fast as lightning.
They leap and dash towards my mouth,
As the commentator says, 'Isn't this exciting?'
I open my mouth to say the winning words,
My tongue flying like little birds,
All of a sudden I start to speak,
My holiday thoughts win the race, but there is a little tweak.
My holiday thoughts cheated along the way,
Oops! I've told the most embarrassing memories!

Eve Shipton (11)
Lothingland Middle School, Lound

Kameo

An element holder
A troll beater
A monster protector
A deep sea swimmer
A family saver
A sprite catcher
A troll slayer
A mass traveller
A beast smasher
An element lover
A shrine saver
An element chaser
A past slayer
A devil killer
An ogre annoyer
A shadow troll killer
An elemental strawberry finder
A health potion finder.

Elliott Nichols (11)
Lothingland Middle School, Lound

Velociraptor

V icious killer
E nchanting creature
L urking predator
O rgan eater
C unning dinosaur
I ron body
R ushing mind
A quick thinker
P ack hunter
T error of the jungle
O utrageous animal
R apid runner.

Taylor Anderson (11)
Lothingland Middle School, Lound

The World

Cars, planes, trucks and vans;
Deathly every one.
You've heard about global warming,
Pollution's no more fun.

Extinct and endangered animals;
Precious every one.
You've heard about pollution,
Extinction's no more fun.

Cans, wire and bubble wrap;
Annoying every one.
You've heard about extinction,
Litter's no more fun.

Each step you take is irreversible,
Every praise and every scowl.
All the things you do and say,
Could help to save our world someday!

Xene Morrison (11)
Lothingland Middle School, Lound

Kameo

A flyer
A monster saver
A deep sea swimmer
A family saver
A troll beater
An element lover
A sly pouncer
A past slayer
A cool elf
A devil slayer
A tree climber
A fruit hunter
A hero.

Adam Conolly (11)
Lothingland Middle School, Lound

My Magic Box
(Based on 'Magic Box' by Kit Wright)

In my magic box I will put . . .
A baby golden Labrador retriever
And a true friend like Lydia Worton.

In my magic box will be . . .
My dream big mansion
And all my friends.

In my magic box will be . . .
My family and £10,000,000
And a piece of gold and silver.

In my magic box will be . . .
A smile from a baby like Xavie,
A bar of chocolate
And a wonderful, pink Mini Cooper.

Emily Gilbert (11)
Lothingland Middle School, Lound

Lip Gloss

She sits there in her sparkly case,
Shimmering in the morning sunlight,
Waiting for me to put her on.
She's glamorous, *glamorous!*
She struts poshly as she reaches my lips,
Grins and smiles at me as she is telling me,
'Put me on, put me on!'
When I slide her sleekly on,
She shines back at me so snobbishly.
She's smart,
She's classy,
She glitters in the sunlight -
A real boyfriend attractor!
A girl's best friend.

Lily Adjemian (10) & Jorden Lewis (11)
Lothingland Middle School, Lound

My Tennis Racket

Oh, my tennis racket,
You are my king,
When you apply top spin to win the match,
A smash serve to ace our opponent,
Oh, you are my ruler!
If you break,
My heart would splinter with you.
When you do a two-handed backhand,
You make it seem so easy.
Oh, my tennis racket,
You are my ecstatic friend.
You make my dreams come true.
Oh, my tennis racket,
If it weren't for you,
My life would be incomplete!

Tom Evans (10)
Lothingland Middle School, Lound

My Magic Box
(Based on 'Magic Box' by Kit Wright)

I will put into the box . . .
The wisdom of magic,
The tail of a Chinese dragon
And the whistle of a harmonic bird.

I will put into the box . . .
A dash of wind from a sprinting cheetah,
A silent swish of a bird diving away
And a friendship that all friends should have.

I will put into the box . . .
A few roses that put a smile on a dull face,
A sleek jump over a whispering crowd,
A happy smile on a hopeful face.

Harrison Broadfoot (11)
Lothingland Middle School, Lound

The Cat - A Haiku

The cat's eyes flare up,
As he sees mice scurrying
Across the carpet.

Quietly he creeps,
His victim is now in sight,
Suddenly he jumps.

Now what have you got?
A small, little, helpless mouse,
Then it . . .
Disappeared!

Bryony Rogers (10)
Lothingland Middle School, Lound

Panda - Cinquain

Panda,
We do love them,
But they're nearly extinct,
Please save them, they don't want to go.
Helpless!

Pandas,
They're really cool,
People hurt them, unfair,
I don't think they feel very safe.
Worried!

Stacey Lambert (11)
Lothingland Middle School, Lound

Kitten

She laps at her milk
As she closes her eyes,
She's always smiling
And when she's finished,
She purrs to get attention.

A tapping of paws
As she runs into the room,
Jumps onto your lap.
You can't help but cuddle her,
Her cute little eyes shining.

Victoria Stone (11)
Lothingland Middle School, Lound

Hamster

A cage climber
A card muncher
A day sleeper
A night walker
A big eater
A fast runner
A mad creature
A non talker
A food nibbler
A cute little pet.

Katie Felgate (11)
Lothingland Middle School, Lound

Dustbin

A food beggar
A crisp cruncher
A strong stander
A rubbish eater
A food swallower
A fox scavenger
A hungry feaster
A sandwich muncher
A garbage disposer
A super gurgler.

William Hilton (11)
Lothingland Middle School, Lound

Heroes Kennings

A life saver,
A match maker,
A secret lover,
A super genius,
A strong lifter,
A girl's dream,
A costume wearer,
A bad guy beater,
A living legend,
A hero!

Charlie Church (11)
Lothingland Middle School, Lound

Cheetah

An animal eater
A good hider
A tree climber
A forest destroyer
A gazelle hunter
A cub protector
A mighty runner
An easy killer
A fierce predator
A mass eater.

Charlie Cassidy (11)
Lothingland Middle School, Lound

Tortoise

A head banger
A slow walker
A shell spinner
A green monster
A lettuce lover
A scary creature
A salad muncher
A fussy eater
A quiet sleeper
A strolling mystery.

Ruby Oldman (11)
Lothingland Middle School, Lound

My Chunky Caterpillar

A transformer
A silent seeker
A gardener's nightmare
An unwanted visitor
A greedy green eater
A veg consumer
A fruit destroyer
A Gunners supporter . . .

My chunky caterpillar.

Regwaan Choudhury (11)
Lothingland Middle School, Lound

Butterfly

B eautiful colours
U nique patterns
T oday a caterpillar
T omorrow a butterfly
E very one different
R eflecting in the sunlight
F lutter by
L anding on a lily
Y oung and wild.

Kate Loveday (11)
Lothingland Middle School, Lound

Nobody

N obody I am
O n the road of life
B lindly through the roads
O nly I know I exist
D o not speak to me
Y ou don't know I exist.

Hannah Illingsworth (11)
Lothingland Middle School, Lound

I'd Rather Be . . .

I'd rather have a door than a gate
I'd rather be called Bobby than Kate
I'd rather try crisps than bait
I'd rather eat from a bowl than a plate
I'd rather be lonely than have a mate
I'd rather eat pizza than After Eights!
I'd rather England win the World Cup than Brazil
That's what I'd hate
That's my life!

Liam Walpole & Liam Clews (11)
Lothingland Middle School, Lound

Snowflake Princess

Slowly she falls and kisses you gently on the cheek.
She twirls and pirouettes round you in her crystal dress.
Shimmering in the moonlight,
She sweeps the grass with her silky dress of ice.
Gracefully, she floats down to you with her glowing cheeks
And blows kisses to the snowmen in her path.
Sadly she trickles away.
Goodbye.

Ewen Keleher (11)
Lothingland Middle School, Lound

Kitten - Cinquain

Kitten
Grows to a cat
Coughs up lots of fluff balls
Starts to miaow for attention
Growing.

Rebecca Reynolds (10)
Lothingland Middle School, Lound

Sky Ride

In the city, in the sun
Tag the wonders that may come
Lots of places to explore
At the park, along the shore
See the world from way up high
It's much nicer in the sky
Grab a balloon from the fair
Soon you'll be flying in the air.

Kirstie Leech (11)
Lothingland Middle School, Lound

The Bee - Cinquain

Spying,
For a red rose,
Where the best nectar is,
Among the other great flowers,
The bee.

Ianthe Harvey (11)
Lothingland Middle School, Lound

Tortoise - Cinquain

Shelly
Slow like a snail
Scaly like a scaly fish
A tiny four-legged reptile
Crawler!

Ashleigh Broughton (11)
Lothingland Middle School, Lound

Spring - Cinquain

In May
New life begins
Flowers shoot from the ground
Baby animals can be seen
Springtime.

Olivia Seago (11)
Lothingland Middle School, Lound

Anger

Anger is a fiery red,
Like a death pit of Hell
Waiting to get me.

It looks like a black hole
Sucking in its prey
And never stops getting bigger.

It sounds like a drip-drop
Thundering through the colossal cave
With darkness above.

It tastes like an
Electric bolt
Of lightning.

It smells like a bubbling swamp
With slimy eels
And more . . .

It feels like a fiery volcano
Waiting
To destroy me.

It reminds me
Of me
Being tormented by the devils of Hell.

Lewis Parsons (10)
Marshlands CP School, Hailsham

Happiness

Happiness is light blue like the sky
Which shimmers in the sunshine
And the waves in the sea
Crashing onto the stony beach.

It sounds like a twittering bird
Singing a sweet tune
Which will echo in my ears
For the rest of eternity.

It smells like a fluorescent waft
Of the bakery as you stroll,
The glorious scent invades your nostrils
Following every step you take.

It tastes like chocolate
Melting slowly in your mouth
Whilst you relax watching a heart-melting film
From the comfort of your sofa.

It feels like smooth velvet
Your fingers slowly drifting over it
And rubbing it raw
Until it is no more.

It looks like a beautiful unicorn
With pure white fur
And a golden mane
With a long, pointy horn.

It reminds me of coloured balloons
Floating in the blue sky
And going pop
When a horrid thing touches it.

Chloe Fudger (10)
Marshlands CP School, Hailsham

Anger!

Anger's colour is like a colossal volcano
Pouring with lava burning my feet.

Anger looks like a burning ball of gas
Heading towards Earth.

Anger sounds like a never-ending earthquake
Bursting my eardrums.

Anger tastes like bitterness, like vinegar
Burning your soul.

Anger smells like a burning bonfire
Which melts my heavy heart.

Anger feels like a meteor rushing to your heart
Ripping it apart.

It reminds me of a colour-blind bull
Charging at my heart.

Tyler Rigglesford (9)
Marshlands CP School, Hailsham

Happiness

Sunshine, daisies, buttercups,
I love the sunshine just as much as you do.

I swim
I see
I see ice cream!

Summer parties, children playing,
Giggles coming near and far.

I smell BBQs in the summer breeze!
My mouth was melting
Full of chocolate
Again and again
No more left!

Maryann Stonestreet (9)
Marshlands CP School, Hailsham

Sadness

Sadness is grey, like a dark, grey day
With misty clouds in the air.

It tastes like salty water
In the drowning sea.

It smells like white lilies
Growing in the shadows.

It looks like a lonely person
Whose heart has broken.

It feels like a knife plunging
In your heart, which is never-ending.

It reminds me of a family member
Dying alone in a cold place.

It sounds like a person
Trying to hold back the tears, whimpering in pain.

Chloe Breeds (11)
Marshlands CP School, Hailsham

Anger

When I got out of bed
All I kept hearing was the toaster popping.
Now it's really getting annoying.

I could feel my blood
Steaming with fire.
I really wish it would stop steaming.

That really keeps annoying me,
My anger smells like little knives
Stabbing into chicken.
Now I really wish it would stop stabbing.

Connor McLaughlan (10)
Marshlands CP School, Hailsham

Anger

When I'm angry, I can only see black,
It also feels like lava on my skin.
I am hotter than the sun
And I can explode better than a bomb.
I can beat any challenge you give me.
In my head I can see red mist.
In my head the red mist is mistier than fog.
In my head I hear an earthquake,
Like the world being split apart.
When I smell, it smells of blood,
It feels like I am a vampire
Sucking someone's blood.
It feels like I am the Titanic
Crashing into an iceberg and sinking.
When I am mad, it reminds me of my little sister
And I calm myself down.

Connor Townsend (9)
Marshlands CP School, Hailsham

Happiness

Happiness is like a white, frothy cat,
Soft, tender to touch,
Dreamy like a block of ice in the breezy wind.
The love-like miaow of a cat
Makes me think of a crystal.

When I'm happy I only see white,
When I think I'm lucky I get hyper
And want water squirted at me.
When I'm happy I feel cool, frozen ice
Like a barrier of snow.

When I'm happy I feel a breeze of wind,
A flash of snow.
I feel jolly I know.

Joseph Hutchinson (10)
Marshlands CP School, Hailsham

Happy

Happiness is a day on the wonderful grass,
Eating lovely ice cream
And sitting down on the beach
Listening to the lovely, beautiful waves.
When I am happy, I can feel
The nice warmth,
But when it gets colder,
I am sad.
The sound is like birds singing
In our heads.

Cherelle McLaughlan (9)
Marshlands CP School, Hailsham

Anger

Anger feels like lava touching my skin.
It also feels like burning fire eating my heart.
It looks like the Devil's horns on my head.
Anger is like a volcano burning away.
Anger smells like unbearable smoke.
Steam is bursting out of my ears and eyes.
It tastes like burning chilli.
It feels like burning in my mouth.
It sounds like screaming rage.

Jason Rogers (10)
Marshlands CP School, Hailsham

Anger

It feels like hot, red lava spilling all over me.
Red mist surrounding me, I just want to punch something.
Red fire burning up in my brain does not stop.
It feels like burning chilli in my mouth.
Anger smells like burning smoke.

Liam Smith (9)
Marshlands CP School, Hailsham

Happiness

When I'm happy I feel like I am at the beach.
When I laugh I hear giggling in my ears and bees buzzing.
I see ice cream, it looks so creamy.
I can taste toffee running down my throat.
I can smell BBQs in the summer breeze.
I feel like I am floating on a candyfloss cloud,
Looking at the summer sky.
In the sea, the summer sun shines on me.

Charlie Williams (9)
Marshlands CP School, Hailsham

Summer Poem

Love is like the sun beaming down,
Love sounds like the birds tweeting,
Love tastes like a bunch of flowers,
Love smells like a blossom tree,
Love looks like a rainbow shining,
Love feels like smooth leaves,
Love reminds me of a snowflake slowly drifting down.

Fun is like laughter of happiness,
Fun sounds like the trees waving,
Fun tastes like roses on a bush,
Fun smells like the love of spring,
Fun looks like the hot, hot sun,
Fun reminds me of my best friend, Hannah
And all my other friends.

Happiness is the colour of the rainbow,
Happiness sounds like a fair going on,
Happiness tastes like spring grass,
Happiness smells like a flower,
Happiness looks like the sun floating,
Happiness feels like the burning sun,
Happiness reminds me of my friend, Tiggy.

Shannon Limberger (8)
Rocks Park Primary School, Uckfield

Under My Bed

Under my bed there's a flesh-eating monster
With hundreds of teeth and claws!!
It waits until it hears my feet,
Then out it comes and roars!

Under my bed there's a flesh-eating monster,
A thing from a mad man's lab!
I really don't know how he got here,
He must have got a cab!

Under my bed there's a flesh-eating monster,
Who's from head to toe dark green!
I know it wants to eat me one day,
For that time it's very keen!

Under my bed there's a flesh-eating monster,
With slippery, slimy scales!
Although this may seem creepy,
It also has eight tails!

Under my bed there's a flesh-eating monster,
An utterly terrible beast!
I know it really wants to eat
But on my body it won't feast!

Under my bed there's a flesh-eating monster,
A creature as tough as can be!
Though it has to stay flat on the ground,
'Cause it doesn't have a knee!

Under my bed there's a flesh-eating monster,
Who ate up my great mate, Terry!
But I'm not frightened of it, oh no,
'Cause it's imaginary!

James Batstone (11)
Rocks Park Primary School, Uckfield

My Sense Poem

Fear is grey like a lonely person,
Fear sounds quite like a test,
Fear tastes disgusting like murky oil,
Fear smells weird like gauva juice,
Fear looks hidden like a lost toy,
Fear feels anxious like an actor about to go on stage,
Fear reminds me of dangerous gangs!

Hate is red like a setting sun,
Hate sounds loud like shouting people,
Hate tastes dull like water,
Hate smells smoky like a raging fire,
Hate looks evil like a monster,
Hate feels shocking like an explosion,
Hate reminds me of a big bully!

Sadness is blue like a running stream,
Sadness sounds like the dripping rain,
Sadness tastes mouldy, like a gone off drink,
Sadness smells salty like the sea,
Sadness looks clear, like the ocean,
Sadness feels slimy like a dripping gutter,
Sadness reminds me of death!

Loneliness is black like the night,
Loneliness sounds quite like a library,
Loneliness tastes horrible like a dirty sandwich,
Loneliness smells like mud,
Loneliness looks like a bare tree,
Loneliness feels spiky like a bush,
Loneliness reminds me of being shouted at!

Kieran Batstone (8)
Rocks Park Primary School, Uckfield

My Sense Poem

Fun is yellow like the beaming sun,
Fun sounds like a winning goal,
Fun tastes like ice cream,
Fun smells like chicken in the greasy oven,
Fun looks like diamonds and rubies
In a box full of gold,
Fun feels like a really big pillow!

Hate is grey, like a dull sky,
Hate sounds like a hundred screams,
Hate tastes like blood in your mouth,
Hate smells like gone off milk,
Hate looks like a big fight,
Hate feels like an alligator's back!

Happiness is like a rainbow full of colours,
Happiness sounds like a baby laughing,
Happiness tastes like a chocolate
In a chocolate fountain,
Happiness smells like buttercups in Kew Gardens,
Happiness looks like a blanket of snow,
Happiness feels like a warm bed!

Anger is red, like flickering ashes off a raging fire,
Anger sounds like a devil's laugh,
Anger tastes like smoky steam coming out of your ears,
Anger smells like a burnt house,
Anger looks like a streak of lightning,
Anger feels like a hedgehog curled in a ball!

Max Goodwin (9)
Rocks Park Primary School, Uckfield

My Sense Poem

Fun is green, like a frog bouncing up and down,
Fun is like the yellow, burning sun,
Fun sounds like people laughing with each other,
Fun tastes like the ice of an iceberg in Antarctica,
Fun smells like burgers on a steaming BBQ,
Fun looks like the shining colours of a rainbow,
Fun feels like the furry fur of a tiger in the jungle!

Happiness is like the greenest grass in the whole world,
Happiness sounds like the music played at a wedding,
Happiness tastes like roasted chicken out of an oven,
Happiness smells like bluebells that have just come out of the ground,
Happiness looks like Mount Everest,
Happiness feels like the petals of a grown sunflower!

Anger is the flames of a raging fire,
Anger sounds like people who are getting aggressive about money,
Anger tastes like sour lemon juice,
Anger smells like steam that comes out of a bonfire,
Anger looks like the Second World War,
Anger feels like lots of knives scattered along the floor!

Hate is grey, like the black sky,
Hate sounds like fireworks set off into the sky,
Hate tastes like blood in your mouth,
Hate looks like steam coming out of somebody's ears,
Hate feels like you've just burnt your hand on the iron!

Harry Limberger (8)
Rocks Park Primary School, Uckfield

If I Could Fly!

If I could fly,
I would soar high in the sky,
I would watch people laugh, cheer and cry,
All the while I fly high in the sky!

If I could fly,
I would scale Mount Everest's mighty peak,
Learning the ancient gods' Greek,
All the while I ascend high in the sky!

If I could fly,
The world's seven wonders I would see,
It never could get tedious for me,
All the while I fly high in the sky!

If I could fly,
I would fulfil all my dreams,
On me the starlight beams,
All the while I ascend high in the sky!

If I could fly,
I would see my local team lift the cup,
Whilst flying up, up, up,
All the while I fly high in the sky!

If I could fly,
I would grow old in the sky,
Fulfilling my destiny I would try,
All the while I ascend high in the sky!

Callum Fuller-Iles (11)
Rocks Park Primary School, Uckfield

My Sense Poem

Fear is black, like the deep night sky,
Fear sounds ferocious, like the howl of a hungry wolf,
Fear tastes burnt like the embers of a fire,
Fear smells smoky like the ashes of a raging fire,
Fear looks evil, like a haunted house,
Fear feels scary, like someone behind you!

Happiness is yellow, like the first light of day,
Happiness sounds like a beautiful choir,
Happiness tastes sweet like honey,
Happiness smells amazing, like fresh cut flowers,
Happiness looks colourful like a field of flowers,
Happiness feels lovely, like a frosty morning!

Love is the deepest red,
Love sounds like a marvellous harp,
Love tastes like rich chocolate cake,
Love smells amazing, like lovely perfume,
Love looks red, like a thousand roses,
Love feels like a never-ending fire inside you!

Fun is the palest blue,
Fun sounds loud like laughing,
Fun tastes heavenly like sweets,
Fun smells like a delicious cake cooking,
Fun looks like a colourful carnival,
Fun feels like a bouncy ball!

Christian Martin (9)
Rocks Park Primary School, Uckfield

I Think My Teacher . . .

I think my teacher lives at school
I think my teacher is an alien
I think my teacher is a mind reader
I think my teacher is a secret agent
But most of all, she encourages *me!*

Karl Milton (11)
Rocks Park Primary School, Uckfield

My Sense Poem

Anger is blazing red like the hot, ferocious sun,
Anger sounds like someone who is very annoyed,
Anger feels electrical like a bolt of lightning,
Anger smells like a big, raging fire,
Anger looks spiky, like a bush of prickly thorns,
Anger feels like a very sore throat!

Fun is light blue like the calm waves of the sea,
Fun sounds like someone crying with laughter,
Fun tastes like a sweet, juicy apple,
Fun smells like a smoky barbecue,
Fun looks like someone screaming with joy on a roller coaster,
Fun feels like bouncing on a squishy, bouncy castle!

Hate is blinding white, like a streak of lighting,
Hate sounds like the piercing noise of an explosion,
Hate tastes like prickly, spiky holly,
Hate smells like a skunk's scent,
Hate looks like people having a noisy argument,
Hate feels like an enormous blue bruise!

Fear is murky brown, like a deserted room,
Fear sounds ruthless, like a piercing scream,
Fear tastes scary, like a pitch-black cupboard,
Fear smells like bright red blood from a cut knee,
Fear feels fast like an agile cheetah,
Fear feels like a broken arm!

Syimyk Kyshtoobaev (9)
Rocks Park Primary School, Uckfield

My Sense Poem

Silence is silver like a scale of a swordfish,
Silence sounds like a bug crawling along,
Silence tastes like the salt of the ocean!
Silence smells like a moth,
Silence feels like a beautiful gem,
Silence looks like a dolphin's fin!

Fun is orange like a bright star,
Fun sounds like the cheers at the Olympic Games,
Fun tastes of food from a barbecue!
Fun smells like a huge fresh fish,
Fun feels like a sheep's wool,
Fun looks like a child!

Happiness is yellow like a big sunflower,
Happiness sounds like a thousand cheers,
Happiness tastes of sugary cinnamon!
Happiness smells of a different dinner,
Happiness feels like the silken hair of a unicorn,
Happiness looks like a huge heart!

Hate is pitch-black like a raging monster,
Hate sounds like insults,
Hate tastes of fiery ashes!
Hate smells of burning petrol,
Hate feels prickly, like the spiky back of a porcupine,
Hate looks like an outraged animal!

Benjamin Ricketts (9)
Rocks Park Primary School, Uckfield

My Sense Poem

Love
Love is red like roses,
Love sounds like a cheer,
Love tastes like the sweetest sponge cake,
Love smells like freshly baked bread,
Love looks like a kiss,
Love feels like a hug,
Love reminds me of a marriage.

Fun
Fun is blue like the sky,
Fun sounds like a cheer of joy,
Fun tastes like toffee bread,
Fun smells like a toffee,
Fun looks like people playing,
Fun feels like a hug of joy,
Fun reminds me of playing.

Sadness
Sadness is black like the night,
Sadness sounds like moaning,
Sadness tastes like mouldy cheese,
Sadness smells like old socks,
Sadness looks like a bolt of lightning,
Sadness feels horrid, like a person crying,
Sadness reminds me of grumpiness.

Jessica Armstrong (8)
Rocks Park Primary School, Uckfield

My Sense Poem

Love is a bright, shimmery, pale pink, like the soft petal of a rose,
Love sounds like the twinkle of a wind chime,
Love tastes delightful, like a sweet cookie,
Love smells like a beautiful lily pad floating on the sparkly water
of a pond,
Love looks like the elegant dancing of a ballerina,
Love feels like the silky feather of an owl,
Love reminds me of a kiss and a hug from my family!

Fun is royal blue like the outstandingly big ocean,
Fun sounds like the laugh of a child,
Fun tastes like a slice of freshly made bread,
Fun smells amazing, like a freshly cut daffodil,
Fun looks like a balloon popping into a million pieces,
Fun feels like a wet blanket of snow,
Fun reminds me of a snowball fight!

Sadness is turquoise like the deep ocean,
Sadness sounds like a fox's cry,
Sadness tastes soft, like a crumbled biscuit,
Sadness smells like a droopy flower,
Sadness looks miserable, like a sobbing child,
Sadness feels like a wet tear,
Sadness reminds me of a child's scream!

Lauren Vane (8)
Rocks Park Primary School, Uckfield

The Human UFOs

The human UFOs go in the windows at night,
Abduct a child, steal some food and silently take flight.
Hiding in lakes to seize unsuspecting water dweller,
Throwing them at people just to annoy the fellas.
They sleep in the day, they're nocturnal you see,
No one knows what they look like, it's a mystery!

Declan Bromfield (10)
Rocks Park Primary School, Uckfield

The Senses

Love is as red as a freshly picked rose,
Love sounds like people laughing with joy on their honeymoon,
Love tastes like a sweet cherry dip,
Love smells like a sweet has burst in my mouth,
Love looks like a tender, divine kiss,
Love feels like a soft koala bear,
Love reminds me of when I got my very own dog!

Fun is as bright as a daisy,
Fun sounds like children skipping,
Fun tastes like a honey cone,
Fun smells like a chocolate chip cookie,
Fun looks like a ray of sunshine,
Fun feels like a soft rug,
Fun reminds me of laughing.

Sadness is as dark as night,
Sadness sounds like a baby crying,
Sadness tastes like salty raindrops dripping slowly yet deadly,
Sadness smells like a pair of smelly shoes,
Sadness looks like a droopy flower,
Sadness feels like a cut inside of you,
Sadness reminds me of my broken teddy bear.

Megan Miles (9)
Rocks Park Primary School, Uckfield

My Sense Poem

Happiness is as blue as the beautiful waves
Crashing against the coastline,
Happiness sounds like children laughing,
Happiness tastes sugary sweet, like a chocolate mousse,
Happiness smells like a freshly cut flower,
Happiness looks like children playing,
Happiness feels like a very furry rug!

Fun is as golden as the rising sun,
Fun sounds like leaves rustling in the breeze,
Fun tastes like heavenly chocolate,
Fun smells like a beautiful tulip,
Fun looks like the twinkling stars,
Fun feels like a baby's soft skin!

Hope is as yellow as a daffodil,
Hope sounds like a baby's first cry,
Hope tastes like a sugar cube,
Hope smells like a chicken roasting,
Hope looks like a beautiful rainbow,
Hope feels smooth, like a very silky cape!

Olivia Baldwin (9)
Rocks Park Primary School, Uckfield

My Sense Poem

Fear sounds like a ghost,
Fear tastes like a cockroach,
Fear smells like poison gas,
Fear looks like a zombie,
Fear feels like a grave,
Fear reminds me of a gremlin!

Hate sounds like a scream,
Hate tastes like the Devil,
Hate smells like smoke,
Hate looks like a witch,
Hate feels like a stone,
Hate reminds me of death!

Happiness sounds like the pitter-patter of rain,
Happiness tastes like a cherry Bakewell,
Happiness smells like roses,
Happiness looks like Heaven,
Happiness feels like a sponge,
Happiness reminds me of smiling!

Luke Oakley (9)
Rocks Park Primary School, Uckfield

Rubbish

Rubbish, rubbish on the ground,
Rubbish, rubbish, always to be found.
Everywhere there is some litter,
Pick it up and put it in the bin
Or you will be caught for a sin.
Rubbish, rubbish, careful where you step,
Rubbish, rubbish, you know where it should be kept.
Rubbish is dirty, rubbish isn't clean,
Some rubbish can just blow up with steam.
Some is poisonous, some is normal,
But most of all, it is more than just rubbish.

Connie Swaysland-Neal (11)
Rocks Park Primary School, Uckfield

My Sense Poem

Silence is pure white, like snow in the middle of winter,
Silence sounds like a butterfly flying across a sweet-smelling garden,
Silence tastes like the salty waters of the ocean,
Silence smells like a soaking wet flower,
Silence looks like a cold day with nothing in sight,
Silence feels like a dew-covered leaf!

Fun is bright yellow like the morning sun,
Fun sounds like children shouting on a summer's day,
Fun tastes like a sweet lollipop,
Fun smells like bacon cooking,
Fun looks like rays of light from the sun,
Fun feels like a sheep's wool!

Happiness is green like freshly cut grass,
Happiness sounds like birds chirping,
Happiness tastes like a chocolate chip cookie,
Happiness smells like a bright red rose,
Happiness looks like a flower-filled meadow,
Happiness feels like a rabbit's fur!

Hannah Baker (9)
Rocks Park Primary School, Uckfield

A Sense Poem

Fun is green, like the freshly cut grass,
Fun is people laughing like excited kookaburras,
Fun is a new cookie baked by an ancient goddess,
Fun is salty like the deep oceans,
Fun is like jumping horses fresh from the stable,
Fun feels like a new spring day,
Fun reminds me of a newborn lamb!

Love is deep red, like a juicy strawberry,
Love is a crab snapping like the jaws of a crocodile,
Love smells like pollen in a rosebud,
Love looks like a pumping heart,
Love reminds me of a special hug!

Anger is pitch-black,
Anger sounds like a wild roar from a hungry lion,
Anger smells like a forever lasting bonfire,
Anger looks really bright, like a flash of lightning,
Anger feels prickly, like a pin in a balloon,
Anger reminds me of somebody shouting!

Chloe Marriott (9)
Rocks Park Primary School, Uckfield

Uckfield Line 150

Eighteen hundred and fifty-eight,
Most certainly an important date.
Locos built by J C Craven
Descended on this country haven,
Followed soon by William Stroudley,
Copper-capped chimneys polished proudly.

There were to follow many others,
A happy band of railway brothers.
Then, along came Dr Beeching,
Bringing changes so far-reaching.
Steam? No thanks.
Thus came the end for standard tanks.

Nineteen hundred and sixty-nine,
They cut the Lewes Uckfield line.
A loyal servant, the Uckfield Thumper
Soldiered on, till all said 'dump her'.
Now they say we can travel afar
By Southern Railway Turbostar.

Ben French (8)
Rocks Park Primary School, Uckfield

My Magic Box
(Based on 'Magic Box' by Kit Wright)

I will put in my box . . .
The sounds of the waves as they hit the shore,
The shine from the summer sun.

I will put in my box . . .
The smell of the flowers from the springtime song of the sun,
The smell of salt and pepper as it goes up my nostrils.

I will put in my box . . .
The smell of freshly cut grass and the feel of long, crisp grass
And the gold of the sand.

My box is fashioned from jewels and precious stones,
Lined with velvet.
It is a dark, heavenly blue.

I shall fly in my box,
To a land of happiness and dreams.
My box was held by the ancient kings and queens,
It has magic dust everywhere.

Millie Hague (9)
Rocks Park Primary School, Uckfield

Today I Heard A Summer Breeze

Today I saw a summer breeze floating in the air,
Water trickling in a stream,
A house being made beam by beam,
A train powered by steam.

Then I saw an autumn gust swirling round and round,
Leaves gently rustling,
Bees hurriedly bustling,
Farmers are tingling.

Next I saw a winter blast whizzing past,
Cold, freezing nights,
Quite a lot of mites,
And many lights!

Last, I felt a spring zephyr brushing on my face,
Animals being born,
The first green shoots of corn,
Sheep being shorn,
All in one year!

Fraser Munn (8)
Rocks Park Primary School, Uckfield

Best Friends!

Friends never leave you unless you tell them to,
They help you and love you through everything you do.
Friends are like a second family,
That's what makes them special.
If they're real friends, they'll never forget you,
Think of one million and one ways to please you.
A true friend is a one in a million chance,
That's what makes them special.
Look after a friend and they'll look after you too,
Forgive and forget all the mean things you do.
Lots of hugs and kisses too,
Forever best friends!

Rachelle Griffith (11)
Rocks Park Primary School, Uckfield

A Sense Poem

Silence is like a bug walking along,
Silence is when someone is asleep,
Silence looks like a clear blue sky,
Silence reminds me of a soft, wavy sea!

Love is romance,
Love looks like red lips,
Love tastes like a piece of tulip,
Love smells like a bowl of peaches,
Love sounds like steaming plates of food,
Love reminds me of red lipstick.

Fun is orange like peaches,
Fun sounds like children giggling,
Fun tastes like chocolate cake,
Fun smells like cakes cooking,
Fun looks like a baby child laughing,
Fun feels like you are very lovely,
Fun reminds me of bunches of tulips.

Elizabeth Trigwell (9)
Rocks Park Primary School, Uckfield

The Stables

As soon as I reach the wooden gate before me,
I can hear the sweet whinnying of horses
Calling desperately to their owners.

As soon as I enter the stable and the barn,
I can smell the pungent, wheaty whiff of chaff and pony treats
Being shut away from the rather plump horses.

As soon as I walk through the flower-carpeted fields,
I see small, gangly-legged foals stumbling through their first steps
And hyper horses fly bucking whilst the sugar lumps kick in.

As soon as I reach the stable and stroke my horse,
I feel our strong bond that just gets stronger every day!

Georgia Lock (11)
Rocks Park Primary School, Uckfield

Springtime

Springtime is full of interest,
Birds and butterflies,
Bees collecting nectar,
Ready for a honey pie.

Springtime is full of interest,
Birds collecting worms,
Squeaking, squawking chicks,
Nearby some wood burns.

Springtime is full of interest,
Bulbs pushing up the earth,
Leaves shooting green and fresh,
Animals giving birth.

Springtime is full of interest,
Lambs skipping around the meadow,
Newborn calves are mooing
And a rabbit in a hollow.

Katie Nettleton (8)
Rocks Park Primary School, Uckfield

My Pet Alien!

He eats all of my Sunday delights
He eats our rubbish in the night
He talks non stop jibberish in his sleep
And he smells like our compost heap

Waterfalls are their fear
Although it dives off Brighton Pier
He's not afraid of my light
But he's allergic if its bright

He will eat a wood and nail sandwich
And his girlfriend is a Hallowe'en witch
So that's my pet alien
Do you have one?

James Munn (11)
Rocks Park Primary School, Uckfield

The Wigglesniggles

Behind the curtains,
Behind the walls,
Live some tiny creatures
Called the Wigglesniggles.

They eat nails for breakfast
And have a very sharp sting,
Four wings of rosy red
And three eyes to see.

They have a poisonous venom
And teeth as blunt as a pencil,
Two mouths to eat
And no stomach to store.

They are nocturnal
And three times smaller than a virus,
Caught by a Venus flytrap
And move at lightning speed.

Stephen Williams (11)
Rocks Park Primary School, Uckfield

My Friend

My friend cares for me,
My friend helps me,
My friend makes me see
That life is a wonderful thing.

My friend makes me laugh,
My friend cheers me up,
My friend sticks up for me,
My friend can give me life.

My friend makes me feel happy,
But that's all wrong because
He's a *monster!*

Harrison Terry (10)
Rocks Park Primary School, Uckfield

Climbing A Mountain!

Nearly at the summit now,
I can almost see the peak,
My fingers and toes are icy cold,
I've been climbing for a week.

My legs feel like they're going to break down
And like I'm going to fall,
It feels like I'm climbing up
A very slippy wall.

I hear the sound of a mighty avalanche
Crashing to the ground,
I'm so happy that now
We've finally found the summit.

I'm so very proud
That we're on the peak,
And now I know
That climbing for a week was worth it!

Ellie Smith (11)
Rocks Park Primary School, Uckfield

Problems

There are so many problems in the world,
Like could you build another Big Ben
Or make your house look like a pig pen?
Could you ever solve these problems?
I couldn't.

There's one more problem in the boo,
But you can solve this problem.
Day by day it's the easiest problem in the book,
You've guessed it, recycling every day.

I get lost in all my problems,
So I hope you don't get lost in my problems.

Matthew Pilcher (10)
Rocks Park Primary School, Uckfield

My Bench

My bench is on top of a grassy, green hill
Where I sit all alone every day after school.
Thinking, watching, having fun,
I sit on my bench under the golden sun.

My bench is under a golden sun,
Surrounded by blue skies, there's only one.
Rising every day to light up the world,
I sit on my bench watching birds fly around.

I sit on my bench watching birds in the air,
I just can't help but sit and stare.
Flapping their wings without any cares,
I sit on my bench on the grassy green hill.

I sit on my bench on the grassy, green hill,
Hoping that I won't catch a chill.
Down below the children play,
While I sit on my bench to watch the world every day.

Alexandra Lane (10)
Rocks Park Primary School, Uckfield

My Pony

My pony is called Bracken,
He is better than the rest,
He is a star when you put him to a test.

My pony is called Bracken,
He is very lazy,
He is as sweet as a daisy.

My pony is called Bracken,
He just loves to eat,
He also likes trotting and never misses a beat!

My pony is called Bracken,
He is dark brown,
He sometimes in a field looks rather like a clown!

My pony is called Bracken,
He canters across the moor,
He slows down to a trot as he sees the tor!

Zaveri Shah-Smith (8)
Rocks Park Primary School, Uckfield

Love

Love can be strong,
Love can be weak,
Love is full of surprises.

Love can be wrong,
Love can be right,
Love is full of happiness.

Love can be late,
Love can be early,
Love is full of excitement.

Love can be busy,
Love can be quiet,
Love is full of anger.

Love can be fun,
Love can be boring,
Love is full of fear.

Sadie Dix (9)
Rocks Park Primary School, Uckfield

Time And Space Traveller

As the mythical man wanders in his machine,
The sound of nothing apart from the trees,
His machine shooting off
Into time and space in the wink of an eye,
Into the past he goes first,
Studying the way they lived,
Being fascinated by the dinosaurs and
The spitting of lava from the active volcanoes.

Rushing to the future now,
Seeing flying cars and spaceships,
Shiny, gold buildings,
It looks like a dream you think of every day,
It is a normal day for him,
But an adventure for us,
How I would love to be the prince
Of the big, wide universe.

Jack Foster (11)
Rocks Park Primary School, Uckfield

Mountains

Soaring in the sky,
Looking up at the rocky mountainside,
Peaks covered in frost,
Thousands of metres high.

Foggy air drifting,
I look up at the gigantic mound,
Dreaming of touching the summit one day,
I would be very proud.

I can hear the sound of screaming people
Begging to come down,
I find the courage to climb the mountain
With all my friends, as a team together,
The summit I touch.

Bethany Maw (10)
Rocks Park Primary School, Uckfield

Excuses, Excuses!

I was doing my homework like I was told,
My handwriting neat, big and bold,
It took me ages to finish and I was glad when I did,
But then in came a stranger,
(A bizarre and unearthly looking kid).
It took one look at my homework and ripped it to shreds,
Then the thing laughed and shook my unsteady wooden bed.
I glared at this annoying little creature,
Focusing on its abnormal and extraordinary features.
Its eyes were green and its cheeks would gleam
And the rest of it was just plain alien!
As I stared at it for so much time,
It suddenly vanished, leaving my ears to chime.
I was standing there not knowing what to do,
When my mum shouted, 'Dinner time! But make sure
Your homework's finished too!'

Abigail Hale (11)
Rocks Park Primary School, Uckfield

My Sense Poem

Fun is like the sun,
Fun feels like the drifting clouds,
Fun sounds like laughter,
Fun looks like a shining yellow,
Fun tastes like chocolate cake.

Happiness is like Liverpool winning the cup,
Happiness sounds like birthdays and cheering,
Happiness tastes like a chocolate fountain,
Happiness feels like fur rubbing my face.

Fear is like a haunted house,
Fear feels dark, spooky and smoky,
Fear tastes like burnt burgers,
Fear sounds like ghosts wandering through the house.

Aston Baden (9)
Rocks Park Primary School, Uckfield

My African Poem

African deserts have bags full of sand,
African deserts have heaps of camels to ride,
African deserts have many people walking miles and miles
For one drop of water,
African deserts have a few mountains.

Africa has wonderful creatures like giraffes with long necks,
Africa has wonderful creatures like the flamingos
Always standing on one leg,
Africa has wonderful creatures like the zebras with their
Black and white stripes,
Africa has wonderful creatures like lions hunting for their prey.

Africa would be warm from the desert,
Africa would be hard to survive in without any water,
Africa would be amazing with all the wonderful creatures there are,
Africa would be a dream to visit.

Claire Robinson (9)
Rocks Park Primary School, Uckfield

Be Eco-Friendly

B e kind to our environment
E arth only lives once

E veryone can play a part to help our world
C ycle as much as you can
O nly we can help our environment

F ood is something you can recycle
R ecycle every day
I hate to see our world destroyed
E verything matters
N ature can be destroyed
D on't throw rubbish on the floor
L andscapes are covered with rubbish
Y ou can change our world.

Charley Baker (11)
Rocks Park Primary School, Uckfield

Sense Poem

Fun:
Fun tastes like a roast chicken being cooked,
Fun sounds like a windy day,
Fun smells like cherries being eaten,
Fun looks like somebody doing funny stuff,
Fun feels like a leaf fight!

Anger:
Anger tastes like a dead baby fox,
Anger sounds like someone shouting,
Anger smells like a black knight.

Fear:
Fear tastes like a ghost haunting a house,
Fear sounds like the sea crashing against the rocks,
Fear smells like someone hiding in the wardrobe!

Rees Rider (9)
Rocks Park Primary School, Uckfield

Night And Day In The Classroom

In the silence the classroom waits
Tables sleeping
Chairs dreaming
The blinds snoring gently
As the wind caresses them.

As the sun rises
The room starts to brighten
Noisy children work
Teachers chatter about the day
Teaching assistants explain when we are not sure
Windows gleaming like the sun
Birds twitter their beautiful song
Clock ticks away
Time to go
We'll be back once more.

Jake Reader (11)
SS Peter & Paul CE Primary School, Bexhill-on-Sea

Seasons Of Beauty

Frost lies white, an icy blanket
And the ice crunches under my feet.
The snow touches me gently,
I am a small person surrounded by white.
My own winter wonderland.

The frost has long ago melted
And daffodils are sprouting up.
The trees are a leafy foliage,
I see flower heads smiling at me.
New life, fresh start, elegance and beauty.

The sky is stretched tight above me,
Cornflower blue.
I run on the white sands.
The sun beams down as the sea laps at my feet.
I could lie here forever basking in the sun.

Leaves are falling, turning somersaults and spinning.
They crackle under my feet.
The floor is carpeted in orange and yellow.
The harvest is plentiful.
Hallowe'en pumpkins leer at me.

The seasons change throughout the year
And so this cycle continues
Year after year after year . . .

May Drawbridge (11)
SS Peter & Paul CE Primary School, Bexhill-on-Sea

Sea Raider

The waves rage and clash into the rocky bed,
The sound of rustling fills the air with excitement,
Feeling on the shore, my heart gets filled more and more,
Their blue layers bare white flesh-eating teeth,
Eventually the waves surrender for a new dawn.

Alexander Clark (11)
SS Peter & Paul CE Primary School, Bexhill-on-Sea

The Summer's Sea

The sea moves in and out,
Boisterous waves crash and shout.
Stand up close, feel the spray,
If only we could stay all day!

Waves are strong, waves are stout,
Waves try to drag the children out.
The smell of doughnuts, tea and coffee,
Ice cream flavours from mint to toffee!

Dogs get wet, dogs have fun,
Bees land on your chocolate bun.
Once you've left, the beach is in a state,
But who's complaining, it's still great!

Early and late, the beach has sand,
The De-La-Warr has hired a band.
People have tea, next to the sea,
Children have fun, full of glee!

The wind wishes willingly for me to go,
It throws us all to and fro,
Pigeons fly, seagulls soar,
I'm away from the beach once more!

Ben Saunders (11)
SS Peter & Paul CE Primary School, Bexhill-on-Sea

The Mansion

Puddles of blood dribbling
Across the entrance hall,
Torn tapestries dress the
Statues.

The corpse of the butler
Attempts to breathe,
Whilst the rats feast on
The flesh and bones.

Samuel Bayliss (11)
SS Peter & Paul CE Primary School, Bexhill-on-Sea

70 Forever

70 years it said
Standing from day to day I do
They come in, they come out
Every second I watched baby Charlotte grow

Cry and cry she did
She crawled, she stumbled, she walked
Saw the change in her face as she grew like a beautiful flower
From pink lips to red lips
Suddenly, she enters a coffin at 70

Listen will you
Hear the music
One day jazz
Another day hip-hop

Still standing
Always standing
Never going anywhere

At least for another 80 years
The De La Warr Pavilion
Alive for the next generation!

Rowena Habadah (11)
SS Peter & Paul CE Primary School, Bexhill-on-Sea

Empty Spaces

Empty spaces
No one around
No one here to hear the sound
Salty seawater spreads on the ground
As the beach starts to wake
People start to come to this place
Children play and run around
Laughter spreads and happiness has begun
It will replay over and over again.

Fiona Rumary (11)
SS Peter & Paul CE Primary School, Bexhill-on-Sea

Splash!

Wind wails,
Thunder rumbles,
Waves crash,
Splash!

Onto the stones,
Cobbled and cracked,
The sea moans, into the black.

Wind wails,
Thunder rumbles,
Waves crash,
Splash!

Calming down,
Restlessness low,
The sea is waiting to say hello.
The sun has risen,
It's time to play,
How many people will come today?

Bethany Claridge (11)
SS Peter & Paul CE Primary School, Bexhill-on-Sea

Cold, Angry Sea

Cold, angry sea,
Crusher of the beach,
Mover of the water,
Moving, living, breathing wrath,
The world's mighty fist of iron,
As permanent as the stars above
But as changing as the air we breathe,
Frothy, white air bubbles tinge the great waves,
The dark sky wraps around you,
Held by your force,
Cold, angry sea,
You beckon me.

Natasha Wilding De Miranda (11)
SS Peter & Paul CE Primary School, Bexhill-on-Sea

Santa

Swooping through the air,
Wind rushing through the chains.
Watching down below,
Amid the mist,
Through the ever-changing world
To get to you.
Over deserts,
Hot and sandy,
Then forests,
Green and noisy.
Across ice,
Cold and weary,
That meet the sea in cliffs . . .

To journey to our homes
And slide down your chimney,
Rushing out before dawn
To make every family jolly.

Joshua Kildea (11)
SS Peter & Paul CE Primary School, Bexhill-on-Sea

Flowers

Flowers so pretty and bright,
Attracting bees when they are in sight,
Any colour - pink, blue, red, purple and yellow,
The nectar as sweet as a marshmallow.

But some flowers are dull,
Like the colour of coal,
The bees leave them alone.

Petals and leaves
Used as decorations on your sleeves.
Dancing in the wind, waving at you,
I bet sometimes they want to say . . .
Boo!

Fleur Lawrie (10)
SS Peter & Paul CE Primary School, Bexhill-on-Sea

A Day In The Park

As I hear feet tumbling,
I lie down under a tree
To watch the birds fly by.
The park will stay here forever.
Every time I visit, it never changes.
I hear children's voices everywhere I turn,
Happiness and laughter everywhere.

As day falls and night arrives,
Everyone leaves for home.
The trees droop as they go away,
At least they enjoyed their stay.

Sparkles on the lake glisten and shine,
As the swans sleep silently
With a cold breeze blowing through their feathers.
They wait patiently.

Amber Cruttenden (11)
SS Peter & Paul CE Primary School, Bexhill-on-Sea

The Sky

The sky flies above our head
It will never go to its bed
Until a late time in the day
When it will turn a gruesome grey
Bold black eats the brilliant blue
It's like it is consuming you
The stars begin to dance across the sky
This process will never die.

After the jet black stops to show
After twelve hours it begins to go
The blue is regurgitated from the black
The light of the sky is coming back
And begins to illuminate the sky
This process will never die.

Liam McGarry (11)
SS Peter & Paul CE Primary School, Bexhill-on-Sea

Dusk To Dawn

The repeating echo of footsteps fills the empty theatre,
Like an ant in a gigantic box, you hunt for an exit but fail.
A cold touch of electrocuting frost sweeps across your cheek,
Whilst an Antarctic iceberg slithers down your straightened spine.
The darkness of the night-time sky surrounds you.
The soul-breaking curse is everywhere.

A peek of a burning star rises from below the deep blue ocean.
The window that separates you from the outside world vanishes,
Then warms the core of your pounding heart.

Finally, the star has brightened the darkness
That lurked around the Earth.
The creeps of the night crawl back to their hideout.
The birds dance whilst singing their graceful harmony.
The theatre has been awakened from its deep sleep.
You're free at last . . . till tonight.

Megan Wilson (11)
SS Peter & Paul CE Primary School, Bexhill-on-Sea

The Beach

The fiery sun rises into the sky
And lights up the deserted beach.
Rays of light pierce through the shadows.

The beach begins to awaken,
Children, parents, grandparents,
All begin to fill the shingle landscape.

As everyone leaves, the storm clouds gather overhead.
The waves gallop around like wild horses,
Crashing into the ageing, wooden groynes.

The storm clouds clear
As the fiery sun sets and disappears
Out of view.

Joshua Ruane (11)
SS Peter & Paul CE Primary School, Bexhill-on-Sea

Arctic Wolf

Dazzling winter sun shines off glaciers,
Wind nips affectionately at his ankles.
Snow crunches like glass,
He brushes trees, who throw a shower of snow at him.
The sun sadly sets,
Winter birds soar, singing.
He watches day dying.

Slowly night creeps, bringing dark, ferocious predators.
The wind taunts him, moaning and howling,
Its smile twisted in malice.
He watches the smiling moon glow,
His fur bristles, hot breath rasping.

Waits,
For day.

Joe Mowbray (10)
SS Peter & Paul CE Primary School, Bexhill-on-Sea

My Ocean

Lapping waves
White horses
Rough strength
Strong, musky
Salty spray
Sea

Calm waves
Silent, deadly
Foaming bubbles
White horses
Glide gently
Sea.

Beth Jeffery (11)
SS Peter & Paul CE Primary School, Bexhill-on-Sea

The Ocean's Day And Night

Raging winds
Blow the salty air,
The stones sit waiting expectantly.
The moonlit water
Shimmers like an earthed star.
Then day breaks,
The shining sun says hello.
The sea is calm as the wind bids its goodbyes.
Chattering crowds make their way down the beach,
Hopping on every stone.
Day has gone and so has the sun,
It's night-time again.

Charlotte Durtnall (11)
SS Peter & Paul CE Primary School, Bexhill-on-Sea

Sand, Stones, Beach, Sun

As I walk along the shore,
The wind, gentle and thick dashes past my face.
The stones, round and hard, crush and crumble underfoot,
As the sea, angry and frustrated, pounds onto the beach.
The sun, strong and hot, beats down like a burning tomato.
The darkness awakens and the sun goes down
And things begin to change.
The storm - striking and straight,
Strikes down on the beach.
The wind, blustery and fast,
Brushes up the stones like a monster, hungry and furious.
And then everything is silent.

Samuel May (11)
SS Peter & Paul CE Primary School, Bexhill-on-Sea

Sea Day And Night

The waves splash and roar
As the eagles soar.
The tide goes in and out
The sea shakes about.
Surfers going up and down
On the waves as they pound.
Then the sun goes down
And darkness is spread all around.
Out come the clouds which start to cry
The storm arises.
The night is full of surprises.

Callum Green (11)
SS Peter & Paul CE Primary School, Bexhill-on-Sea

Sea At Night

The clouds are mean,
The moon comes out,
Night has come,
No people about,
Crashing against the ragged, grey rocks,
The sea is angry,
Lightning cracks,
The white horses are shown,
Angry looks,
Stones being thrown,
This is the sea at night-time as known.

Eloise Jeffery (11)
SS Peter & Paul CE Primary School, Bexhill-on-Sea

Easter Time

This is Jesus' story
He is the King of glory
He died on the cross
And into the world a great loss
Jesus died because
Peter, not once, not twice, three times he lied
Easter can be sunny
And if you're lucky you might get money
We have Easter eggs and hot cross buns
That's what makes Easter *fun!*

Lucy Tucknott (11)
SS Peter & Paul CE Primary School, Bexhill-on-Sea

The Beach

The morning sun awakens
As the stones upon the beach weaken.
When the sun moves across the sky,
Hear the lonely sea cry.

At noon the sun brightens,
I hear movement and laughter.
The children swim, shout and run about.

It darkens,
The waves whisper, *'Night-night.'*

Emma Rushbrooke (11)
SS Peter & Paul CE Primary School, Bexhill-on-Sea

Space

I am in a deep, dark, dull place.
It is a large, plain, empty space.
Feeling lonely and very scared
As if no one in the world cared.

Simon Richardson (10)
SS Peter & Paul CE Primary School, Bexhill-on-Sea

The Blue Sea

Loud noises,
Waves splashing,
The wind brushing across your face,
The smell of salty air filling up your nose,
The calm, peaceful, relaxing sea,
But no one is here to hear the sound of waves crashing,
Its gentle sound.

Ben Smith (10)
SS Peter & Paul CE Primary School, Bexhill-on-Sea

The Sun

The sun starts to rise in the east,
Mild at first, then as bright as a firework,
Winds try to fight the big ball of fire,
The rain falls and calls to the heavens.
I wish that orange ball of fun would come back to my world.
As night falls, the sun sleeps,
I cannot wait until I feel its morning heat!

Amy Izzard (11)
SS Peter & Paul CE Primary School, Bexhill-on-Sea

The Tender Sea

Waves splash, wind whistles as it rushes through
My greasy, thick hair.
A smell so salty, you can taste it in the air.
Whilst the sea's greeny-blue waves stop, another starts
But a single wave can never last!
The sound is kept forever ongoing.
We all are forever knowing.

Max Woolfrey (11)
SS Peter & Paul CE Primary School, Bexhill-on-Sea

Poetry Explorers 2009 - The East & South East England

Time Going By

I can feel the breeze pushing on my cheek,
The sea crashing down like a stone,
The smell of salt in the air,
It's getting darker
And the sea is getting more furious.
I can only hear the waves and I can only see the darkness.

Linley Ross (11)
SS Peter & Paul CE Primary School, Bexhill-on-Sea

The Sea

The vicious sea crashes down
Onto the dull rocks as the sea calms down.
Children play in the gentle blue sea.
As the sun goes down, night spreads all around.
As the sun sleeps,
The moon comes into the starry sky!

Ben Flenley (11)
SS Peter & Paul CE Primary School, Bexhill-on-Sea

The Flower Meadow

The flower meadow is bright yellow, pink, blue and red too.
There are roses and daffodils, bluebells as well,
There, daffodils smell twice as good.
Bees go flower to flower, pollination is in the air.
Nature is there; bees, butterflies and rabbits, deer too.
The flower meadow.

Maartje Deeprose (11)
SS Peter & Paul CE Primary School, Bexhill-on-Sea

Wonderful Sea

The wavy water crashes against the stony shore
And then retreats back to the loud-tempered sea.
The salt runs between the wet stones, never to be moved back.
I smell the salty air filling my lungs with fresh oxygen.
The sea is an amazing place where lots of history hits your face
And opens a gate of imagination because the sea is truly great.

Simon Tomlinson (11)
SS Peter & Paul CE Primary School, Bexhill-on-Sea

The Ocean

Oh, what a day, looking at the spray
From the white sea horses galloping along the waves.
I can smell the huge ocean,
I can hear the sea waves crashing down on the stones
Lying on the seabed,
I can feel the cold ocean breeze stroke my face.

Tom Eden (11)
SS Peter & Paul CE Primary School, Bexhill-on-Sea

Springtime Beach

Stony, sandy waves crash down
Lumpy, bumpy in the ice-cold sand
As the surf comes towards me, I shiver in the ice-cold
Wind whistles all around
We come to a stop
There's a smooth opening to the morning.

Amber Stubbs (10)
SS Peter & Paul CE Primary School, Bexhill-on-Sea

The Fierce Sea

Rough, tough in the very fierce sea
Blue, grey and green are the colours of the water
Waves come crashing down on the stones
The breeze pushes against the sea
It moves backwards and forwards in a very strange way
If the wind gets more fierce it could blow me away.

Adele Vincent (11)
SS Peter & Paul CE Primary School, Bexhill-on-Sea

The Sea

The tide is fierce, white and blue,
It came in and out as the time flew,
You will get wet if you don't frown
But it's a wonderful landscape for us to walk down.
But in the end we're sitting at the table,
Eating chocolate chip mint Cornetto!

Reece Beard (11)
SS Peter & Paul CE Primary School, Bexhill-on-Sea

The Seaside

The sound of the waves just comes and goes.
The seagulls call for their family as the waves crash on the stones.
The wind blows my hair back and forth as all the people walk by.
The pebbles just sit there watching me.
Some of the salty sea spray touches my tongue.

Emily Hobbs (10)
SS Peter & Paul CE Primary School, Bexhill-on-Sea

Sea

Rough, calm
The white horses gallop through the flooding
Always there
Close yet far
The sea will never disappear.

Reilly McDonnell (11)
SS Peter & Paul CE Primary School, Bexhill-on-Sea

As Time Changes

I can feel the ferocious wind blowing against me.
I can smell the salty air,
The waves crashing against the beach.
As dark falls and the sea gets fiercer,
As the tide comes in and out.

George Robinson (11)
SS Peter & Paul CE Primary School, Bexhill-on-Sea

Sea

S ea is calm and full of joy
E ating ice cream at the beach
A nd the sun is boiling.

Louis Wicks (10)
SS Peter & Paul CE Primary School, Bexhill-on-Sea

Sea

S pectacular place
E arth is covered with it
A bsolutely great.

Archie Whittaker (11)
SS Peter & Paul CE Primary School, Bexhill-on-Sea

Kieran's Beach

I can hear the waves crashing on the beach,
The wind blowing against my face non-stop.
I can smell the salty water as I sit on the beach.

Kieran Inglis (11)
SS Peter & Paul CE Primary School, Bexhill-on-Sea

My Secret Place

My secret place has got trees and sparkly lights
And a little place for me to hang my kites
When I go there I call for my best friend
Who lives just around the bend
She and I, we sit and wait until we're tired
Because it's getting late when I say goodbye to her
And then it's time for bed
I pack up all the stuff and shove it in the shed
In the morning I go back to my secret place
My mum's sitting there, I see her face to face
Tomorrow maybe you'll see me
But now I'm going to go home
'Cause I want to catch a bee!

Shelby Haynes (10)
St Helen's CP School, Ipswich

Feelings

Happiness is remembering my great grandfather
Who saved our country
Happiness tastes like a bright blue cake with
Bright purple icing dripping down it
Happiness smells like buttercups in a field
Happiness looks like my cousin in Trowbridge
Happiness sounds like horses' clip-clopping feet
Happiness feels like my soft, cuddly brother.

Maia Shouksmith (8)
St Helen's CP School, Ipswich

My Friend

A friendly, helpful person
A caring, kind person
A sharing, truthful person
A trustworthy, friendship person
An easy, funny person
A fun, fabulous person
A fair, fearless person
A sociable, easy to get on with person
An easy-going, agreeable person
A lucky, warm effect
An outgoing, affectionate person
A relaxed, informal person
A good-natured, cordial person.

Hafizur Hussain Ullah (10)
St Helen's CP School, Ipswich

My Dog Storm

He is as fast as lightning
Sometimes he's frightening
He is very fat
And often sleeps on a mat
He is brown and white
And not very bright
He will eat anything
Because his favourite hobby is eating
He is friends with my rabbit
He doesn't drool
Because he's cool.

Lee Thorpe (11)
St Helen's CP School, Ipswich

Friends

Advice-giver
Friendly-hugger
Truth-teller
Tear-stopper
Smile-creator
Tear-dryer
Problem-solver
Heart-mender
Great companion
A friend!

Katy Jane Forrester (11)
St Helen's CP School, Ipswich

A Football Player

Best shooter
A good goalie
A fine player
A cool team player
A diva diver
A friendly player
A good trapper
A great passer
A large kick
A magic save.

Charlie-Louise Parker (9)
St Helen's CP School, Ipswich

Friends

F un and happy all the time
R eady to play throughout the day
I f your friends are true, they will always help you
E very day of every week of every year
N ever will they let a fear
D rown the friendship that you have
S o enjoy it because you can!

Charlie Woodage (10)
St Helen's CP School, Ipswich

My Feelings

Happiness is blue, as blue as the sky
Happiness tastes like my brother's yummy
Scrummy Spider-Man cake
Happiness smells like six burgers cooking on an oven
Happiness looks like a prince saving the day!
Happiness sounds like a lion carer cutting the grass
Happiness feels like cuddling my mum.

Mohammed Imran (8)
St Helen's CP School, Ipswich

People

Pet-keeper
Machine-maker
Animal-killer
Rainforest-cutter
Sound-speaker
Earth-killer
Food-maker.

Jack Iddon (11)
St Helen's CP School, Ipswich

Senses

Happiness is blue, blue as the ocean
Happiness tastes like pizza just out of the oven and roast dinner
Happiness feels like a hot spotlight from a play
Happiness feels like a bumpy rock at the seaside
Happiness smells like fish and chips
Happiness is watching the sunset.

Ines Bowman-Boyles (7)
St Helen's CP School, Ipswich

My Feelings

Happiness is pink, pink as my favourite pink dress
Happiness taste like when my mum made me cookies
Happiness smells like fabulous fragrant flowers
Happiness sounds like songs sung on a beautiful sunny day
Happiness looks like my sister smiling
Happiness feels like I am smiling with my family.

Anushka Ghiya (8)
St Helen's CP School, Ipswich

My Happiness

Happiness is like a sneaky spy tip toeing around their rooms
Happiness tastes like a sundae dripping down my throat
Happiness looks like an ice skater going really fast
Happiness sounds like the bangers going off on Firework Night
Happiness smells like the lovely sea
Happiness feels like a lovely kitten rubbing against my cheek.

Broghan Ellis (8)
St Helen's CP School, Ipswich

Feelings

Happiness is playing on the computer
Happiness tastes like cucumber and carrot
Happiness smells like chocolate mousse
Happiness looks like the stars shining down on town
Happiness sounds like trumpets playing
Happiness feels like my cuddly toy.

Perran Hugo King (7)
St Helen's CP School, Ipswich

Worries

Everybody worries,
I worry,
You worry,
Everybody worries.
But what do kids worry about?
Bullies?
Scary teachers?
New school?
New house?
Burglars?
But what's the need to worry?
It just wastes time and energy.

So I worry,
You worry,
Everybody worries.
What do adults worry about?
Losing jobs?
Having no money?
Not being able to feed their family?
New house?
New neighbourhood?
I don't know what you worry about
But I worry about my school dinners, *sometimes!*

Katherine Hurley (10)
St Helen's CP School, Ipswich

The Dragonfly

How elegantly the dragonfly hovers
Around the humans
Who don't give a bother.
But he wasn't always like this,
A beautiful bug,
He used to be a beast,
A fault in creation.

They hunt anything near them
And do it standing still,
So the whole pond fears him
And can never seem to chill.

Unfortunately,
He didn't want to be a beast
But it was nature
To say the least.

But one day,
He had the need
To leave the pond
And climb up a reed.

And suddenly an invisible knife
Sliced his back,
Then a beautiful bug
Broke free from his cage
And flew off
To enjoy the rest of his life.

Felix Todd (10)
St Helen's CP School, Ipswich

The Friend

So beautiful
So lovely
So nice
So kind
So helpful
So gorgeous
So cheerful
Likes rainbows
So crazy
So mad
So hyper
Golden heart
Rainbow tears
Silver eyes
Wild hair
Black as night
So lazy
So funny
So fast
Loves cats
Loves dogs
Loves me.

Naia Brown-Powell (9)
St Helen's CP School, Ipswich

Feelings

Happiness is remembering my great, great, great granny who saved our country.
Happiness tastes like McDonald's.
Happiness smells like bright red poppies growing in the field.
Happiness looks like seeing my grandad because he lives a long way away.
Happiness sounds like people's feet still going past me in the street.
Happiness feels like touching my teddy.

Hannah Noble (7)
St Helen's CP School, Ipswich

My Dog

Funny snorer,
Human lover,
Greedy guts,
Attention seeker,
Lazy sleeper,
Fast walker,
Chubby cheeks,
Fly chaser,
Lead puller,
Big cuddler,
Cheeky monkey,
Loud barker,
Wide yawner,
Big hiccups,
High jumper,
Clumsy face,
Busy sniffer,
He is a naughty boy, but he is the best!

Louisa Pisaturo (8)
St Helen's CP School, Ipswich

Esther

Best friend,
Cute girl,
Noisy chatter,
Best gymnast,
Fast runner,
High jumper,
Mad person,
Cheeky monkey,
Good swimmer,
Cool hair bands,
Sweet freckles,
Neat writer.

Rhiannon Lugo (9)
St Helen's CP School, Ipswich

The Hum-Minder

School's ended,
Everyone's at home,
They're out and about,
Not alone.

When the clock strikes 12,
She's ready and out,
Here comes the Hum-Minder,
Watch out!

She creeps through the corridors,
She plays with the sand,
She dances alone,
With an imaginary band.

When the clock strikes 7,
She's out again,
Waiting to invade
Another school again.

Alima Aktar (11)
St Helen's CP School, Ipswich

The Bully

Big head
Fat man
Big boy
Tough man
Strong man
Joker
Loud mouth
Chatterbox
Messy eater
Teacher pusher
Black dresser
Villain
Not cool dude.

Rishawn Mohamed (8)
St Helen's CP School, Ipswich

My Dog

Cheeky minx,
Kissy girl,
Fast runner,
Greedy guts,
Snail eater,
Chubby cheeks,
Lead puller,
Silly yapper,
Little nibbler,
Loud yawner,
Sleepy eyes,
Breaking out,
Head locker,
Bee chaser,
All this, but I still love her to bits.

Daisy Bissett (9)
St Helen's CP School, Ipswich

My Cat, Olive

Lazy sleeper,
Mouse killer,
Greedy guts,
Sleepy eyes,
Attention seeker,
Bee chaser,
Chubby cheeks,
Loud miaower,
Fluffy ball,
Cute cuddler,
Frisky friend,
Wide yawner,
Mucky pup

And I love her to bits!

Dora Densham Bond (9)
St Helen's CP School, Ipswich

I'm Sorry

I'm sorry to say
Your bike flew away

I'm sorry to say
That you're quite annoying today

I'm sorry to say
You turned into a banana yesterday

I'm sorry to say
You stood in goal today

I'm sorry to say
But did you run away?

I'm sorry to say
But I'm going on holiday today!

Jordan Romero (11)
St Helen's CP School, Ipswich

My Cat, Tom

Soft-hearted,
Scampers about,
Funny clown,
Messy eater,
Lovely boy,
Buggy sitter,
Fun kitty,
Fluffy ball,
Sharp claws,
Long legs,
Bushy tail,
Loving eyes;

That was many years ago.

Natasha Smith (9)
St Helen's CP School, Ipswich

My Goldfish, Goldie

Cheeky eater,
Gentle friend,
Chubby cheeks,
Wild fighter,
Cool dude,
Messy chewer,
Noisy swimmer,
Clumsy fish,
Big girl,
Cheeky sleeper,
Chubby cheeks.

All this naughty stuff,
But I love her to bits!

Chloe Hickman (9)
St Helen's CP School, Ipswich

All Four Seasons

Spring:
Bright yellow daffodil bulbs going *boing*
Rhubarb going crumbly with soft cream
Summer:
Colourful berries being smoothied
Sweetcorn being butterly bathed
Autumn:
Sweetened apples stuffing pies
Tomatoes getting saucy
Winter:
Cabbage bubble and squeaks
Pumpkins squashed into a fresh, tasty soup
What a whole exhilarating year we can eat!

Willow Kirkby (11)
St Helen's CP School, Ipswich

I'm Sorry To Say

I'm sorry to say
Your bird flew away,
I'm sorry to say
I can't play today.

I'm sorry to say
You had a rubbish birthday,
I'm sorry to say
That you got beat up yesterday.

I'm not sorry to say
I'm going on holiday.
Good day!

Will Disney (11)
St Helen's CP School, Ipswich

My Dog, Archie

A letter chewer,
A lead puller,
A high jumper,
A postman chaser,
A fast runner,
A loud barker,
A shoe chewer,
A hairy racer,
A tiny yapper,
A tail chaser.

That's Archie.

Liam Roberts (9)
St Helen's CP School, Ipswich

The Star

In the night
It shines so bright,
It's so beautiful
It's got a pretty heart,
It's got a golden shape,
Lives in the sky,
It has a life in the air,
Floating in the night,
With the sun it doesn't shine so bright,
With the moon it's so sparkling,
Goodnight everyone, goodbye.

Kassandra Hamm (9)
St Helen's CP School, Ipswich

I Like To See Your Smile

I see the crystal sea
The sky is light blue
I want to see you
You smell like cherries
Like music to my ears
You are the sun
Lighting up bright
I like to see your smile
In the morning
You shine up the night in your gloom.

Bailey Robinson (9)
St Helen's CP School, Ipswich

Would You Rather?

Would you rather be eaten by lions or by ants?
Would you rather eat dirt or pants?
What about fight a scary cat or be savaged by a wombat?
Would you rather smell of sweat or have to put your house to let?
Would you rather breathe like Vader or talk like Yoda?
Would you rather wrestle a bear or do exhausting yoga?
Would you rather say half empty or half full?
Would you like to live it all or would you never even try to pull
Yourself into fun, or would you sit and eat a bun?
Would you like to use your mind or let it stop and *grind*?

Harry Holian (11)
St Helen's CP School, Ipswich

My Kitten

Strong boy,
Fearless friend,
Tiny body,
Milk lover,
Furry kid,
Sleepy kitten,
Purring baby,
Swimming hater.

He is mine!

Chloe Parkin (9)
St Helen's CP School, Ipswich

Aliens

Aliens
Scary, funky,
Gloomy, freaky, fat,
They are green and slimy too,
Argh!

Charlotte Simms (9)
St Helen's CP School, Ipswich

Man United

M an U rule, we won the Prem
A lex Ferguson is the king
N ani, the speeding bullet

U nited are the most successful team in England
N erve-wracking scores worrying the manager
I nternational club World Cup winners
T evez the late hero
E vra the best left back in the world
D ear Liverpool, Man U rule.

Andrew Chenery (10)
St Helen's CP School, Ipswich

Little Laureates

Friendly,
Scary,
Sometimes hairy,
Little Laureates is full of poems,
Different types you will find,
Maybe mine will be there,
But I mean in the book of course,
Like a bird I will fly
If my poem gets in the book!

Ellen Lear (10)
St Helen's CP School, Ipswich

Speedy

S pecial as the Crown jewels
P recious as a house of gold
E nergetic as a newly trained athlete
E nthusiastic eater
D aring as a person scuba-diving with a shark
Y ou can't get a better pet.

Shumie Akhtar (11)
St Helen's CP School, Ipswich

A Racing Car

A sharp shooter,
A tyre smoker,
A sound maker,
A bursting exhaust pipe,
A flaming wheel,
A rusty engine,
A friction burner,
A blistering tyre,
A rapid driver.

Nasim Miah (9)
St Helen's CP School, Ipswich

Fireworks

F laming bursts of colour
I watch them illuminate the sky
R ed, green, blue, yellow
E very colour of the rainbow
W hy do they explode like that?
O range, silver, gold, purple
R oaring with glee, triumphantly
K aleidoscopic colours beaming
S tars in the sky envy them.

Samuel Clarke (11)
St Helen's CP School, Ipswich

My Best Family Is . . .

Huge, enjoyable, crazy, mad,
Friendly, kind, helpful, funny,
Silly, gleeful, flat, dull, boring, noisy,
Shouty, painful, ill,
Lastly,
Best family ever!

Halima Sultana (9)
St Helen's CP School, Ipswich

My Friend

Kind-hearted,
Friendly chatterbox,
Chatty person,
Funny clown,
Blonde girl,
Best drawer,
Strong-handed,
Short fringed,
Prettiest clothes.

Kirsty Simms (9)
St Helen's CP School, Ipswich

My Gerbil

Fast runner
Peanut eater
Tube climber
Cardboard gnawer
Sound sleeper
Sharp biter
Wood destroyer
Invisible hider
Firm gripper.

William Stewart (9)
St Helen's CP School, Ipswich

Footballer

Good player
Keen trainer
Good skiller
Wonderful goalie
Best trophies
Best team.

Afjal Miah (9)
St Helen's CP School, Ipswich

Mermaids' Purses

Silly fishes lay their eggs
Where greedy jaws can eat them,
But dogfish pop their eggs in pods
And kindly mermaids find them.

The mermaids hide the pods away
From hungry birds and beaks,
Until the baby fishes hatch,
(They wait for weeks and weeks).

Farjana Aktar (9)
St Helen's CP School, Ipswich

My Dog

Strong defender,
Fearsome fighter,
Mega barker,
Overtaker,
Super speeder,
Vampire slayer,
Extreme swimmer.

My pet!

Baker Kagimu (9)
St Helen's CP School, Ipswich

Boredom And Excitement

Boredom
Tired, transparent
Sitting, watching, leaving
Smells like water, feels like a spring
Climbing, laughing, jumping
Amazing, fun
Excitement.

Priyanka Bikkannavar (9)
St Helen's CP School, Ipswich

Gymnast

Fast flipper,
Loud skipper,
Long vaulter,
High jumper,
Toe toucher,
Leg spinner,
Fun flicker,
Cute girl.

Esther Noble (9)
St Helen's CP School, Ipswich

My Chair

It feels as soft as a pillow,
It feels as squishy as a ball,
It sounds as noisy as a dog,
It's as smelly as Lynx,
I cuddle up and go to sleep,
It feels as warm as the sun,
It feels as cuddly as a teddy,
It is as smooth as silk.

Samuel Clarkson (9)
St Helen's CP School, Ipswich

Snowman

Snow white
Fun maker
Pointy nose
Warm scarf
Pointy fingers
No legs
Big tummy
Cold snow.

Jack Butler Pearson (9)
St Helen's CP School, Ipswich

The Bully

Shoplifter,
Punching maniac,
Cash stealer,
Strong man,
Fat face,
Playground torturer,
Evil villain,
Scratchy boy.

Sam Jones (9)
St Helen's CP School, Ipswich

My Friend

Kind and helpful,
Friendly buddy,
Very chatty,
Annoying at times,
But nice always,
Funny clown,
Good mate,
Trusting and reliable.

Arifha Aktar (9)
St Helen's CP School, Ipswich

Cats

A soft cushion
A fast chaser
A leading pet
A gorgeous purrer
A sensitive baby
Cuddly as cotton
A small purrer
A person hugger.

Rebecca Lewis (9)
St Helen's CP School, Ipswich

Pokémon

P ikachu, the most popular Pokémon produces preposterous, electric levels
O nix, the fighting fantasy, punching people senseless
K ing of grass Pokémon, Shaymin, the gratitude Pokémon
E mpoleon, peruser of the vast sea, the water wonder
M ew, mystery origins, unknown as to its true nature
O mighty Charizard, flaming, fantastic and fiery,
N idoking, the normal beginnings of imagination!

Kean Fry (11)
St Helen's CP School, Ipswich

Homo-Sapiens

World obliterators
Technology creators
Habitat demolishers
Pet guardians
Animal consumers
Freedom embracers
Tree abolishers
Extinction preventers.

Moya-Alice Bowman (11)
St Helen's CP School, Ipswich

Snow

Snow is white
It feels like you are riding on Santa
It tastes like an ice cream
It smells like white milk
It sounds like a roaring polar bear
I like the snow because we build snowmen
And we throw snowballs.

John Monge (9)
St Helen's CP School, Ipswich

A Racing Car

A tyre scorcher
A noise maker
A blistering tyre
A supersonic turbo boost
A flaming colour
A smoking wheel
A scorching booster.

Nadir Islam (10)
St Helen's CP School, Ipswich

The Bully

Big meanie,
Fighting machine,
Tough tiger,
Super bling,
Mind of money,
Heart of devil,
Devil ways.

Lindsey Page-Mason (9)
St Helen's CP School, Ipswich

Colours

Rouge at the top, shines like a treasure,
Pound coin yellow making the human race joyful,
Orange, the colour that crabs are proud of,
Sea-green frogs leaping from rock to rock,
Azure sky smiling as the rain clouds gather,
Coral roses bloom in the sunlight,
Surrounding us, colours are everywhere.

Sophie Turner (10)
St Helen's CP School, Ipswich

My Friend

My friend looks like a prancing pony in a poppy field.
She sounds like happy laughter at a party.
She smells like cherries in a fruit bowl.
She tastes like melted chocolate being poured onto cake.
She feels like a bouncy silk pillow on a soft velvet sofa.
That's my best friend.

Molly Gooding (9)
St Helen's CP School, Ipswich

My Guinea Pig

Big, black
Very cute
Super fast
Exceedingly strong
Firm gripper
Extremely wriggly.

Jacob Kirkby (8)
St Helen's CP School, Ipswich

My Cat

A fluffy bunny
A striped tiger
A bird killer
A running cheetah
A chasing lion
A street walker.

Clare Parker (10)
St Helen's CP School, Ipswich

Poppy Power

Soft pup
Cute and cuddly
Mad about food
Very cheeky
Waggy tail
And noisy.

Amy Goodger (9)
St Helen's CP School, Ipswich

Happiness

Happiness is yellow, as yellow as my cuddly bear.
Happiness tastes like a lovely roast dinner.
Happiness smells like flowers growing on the green grass.
Happiness looks like a duck swimming in the pond.
Happiness sounds like a bird chirping in the tree.
Happiness feels like a bird hatching from its egg.

Sian Chapman (8)
St Helen's CP School, Ipswich

Feelings

Happiness is as blue as the beautiful, bobbly blue sea
Happiness tastes like jelly with sprinkles
Happiness smells like flowers growing in the sunset
Happiness looks like the butterflies are singing on the tree
Happiness sounds like the dolphins are jumping in the sea
Happiness feels like a cat relaxing.

Faimah Sultana (7)
St Helen's CP School, Ipswich

Speedy The Cat

Human chaser,
Friend puller,
Annoying moaner,
Noisy snorer,
Loud miaower.

Musomie Aktar (8)
St Helen's CP School, Ipswich

Jake The German Shepherd Dog

He is fierce
He is a show chewer
He is strong
He is speedy like a cheetah
He is friendly like a cat.

Owen Miller (10)
St Helen's CP School, Ipswich

Guinea Pig

Fluffy, cute
Squeaking, biting, shivering
Happy when you cuddle it
Albino.

Chloe Watson-Boyle (9)
St Helen's CP School, Ipswich

Halfway Down The Alleyway

Halfway down the alleyway
I met a cat called Lizzie
We barely got a minute to speak
Cos sadly she was busy.

Halfway down the alleyway
I met a cat called Jean
She looked just like a friendly cat
But really she was mean.

Halfway down the alleyway
I met a cat called Billy
He looked at me, I ran away
But then I felt so silly.

Halfway down the alleyway
I met a cat called Jake
He had those kind of pointy ears
And a long black tail like a snake.

Halfway down the alleyway
I met a cat called Phil
All his fur had fallen out
He told me he felt ill.

Halfway down the alleyway
I met a cat called John
One minute he was there
The next he was gone.

Halfway down the alleyway
I met a cat called Jane
She spat at me, she shook her tail
She's really quite a pain.

Halfway down the alleyway
I met a cat called Fred
This is where my poem ends
Cos sadly he was dead!

Eleanor Hitchings (9)
St John's CE (VA) Primary School, Ipswich

There's A Monster In My Cupboard

There's a monster in my cupboard, nobody cares
He has pink curly monster hairs.

Come on everybody, look inside
I've seen him with my own human eyes
He is spotty, his hair's knotty
With a blue moustache
And he has a very scary roar!

He is hiding in my cupboard, nobody knows
He has really long red monster toes.

Come on everybody, look inside
I've seen him with my own human eyes
He is spotty, his hair's knotty
With a blue moustache
And he has a very scary roar!

He is undercover in there, nobody believes me
He has round orange monster knees.

Come on everybody, look inside
I've seen him with my own human eyes
He is spotty, his hair's knotty
With a blue moustache
And he has a very scary roar!

Everyone thinks I'm crazy
Everyone thinks I'm a fool
That's why my monster came to call
And scared you with his roar!

Amelia Calderhead (10)
St John's CE (VA) Primary School, Ipswich

I Can See A Smelly Sock!

I can see a smelly sock
I wonder whose it is?
I asked my dad if he knew
But he said it wasn't his.

I can see a smelly sock
I think it could be Mum's
But when I went to ask her
She said, 'It isn't mine that
Hums.'

I can see a smelly sock
It must be my sister Lu's
She said it doesn't belong to her
So I'm running out of clues.

I can see a smelly sock
My big sister's feet do pong
She says she doesn't wear that size
So I think I must be wrong.

I can see a smelly sock
It looks about my size
I think I'll take a closer look
I can't believe my eyes.

I can see a smelly sock
I look at it and stare
It's the one that I've been missing
From my favourite smelly pair.

Oliver Page (9)
St John's CE (VA) Primary School, Ipswich

Whatever The Weather

Whatever the weather
Whenever the weather
Whether rain or snow
We don't really know
We're always gonna have fun.

When it's pouring with rain
We go outside again
With our umbrellas
We're happy fellas
We're gonna have fun again.

Whatever the weather
Whenever the weather
Whether rain or snow
We don't really know
We're always gonna have fun.

When the sun is out
We get up and about
Every single day
Hope it stays today
We're gonna have fun again.

Whatever the weather
Whenever the weather
Whether rain or snow
We don't really know
We're always gonna have fun.

Ryan O'Shea (9)
St John's CE (VA) Primary School, Ipswich

I Sense A Storm

As windy as a fan on high
Gusting clouds across the sky
As I look up and wonder why
A drop of rain falls in my eye.

The clouds become a swirling froth
The sky a frame of blackened cloth
Out of nowhere a flash appears
And thunder echoes in my ears.

The trees, their arms in disarray
Leaves like ants trying to find their way
Rain pouring as if from a hose
The smell of lightning in my nose.

The water in the drains is rushing away
To be used by us some other day
At least this won't go to waste
Even if it isn't to everyone's taste.

All of a sudden the wind disappears
And the rain puts away its vicious spears
I'm not concerned with this so much
As the sun popping out to stay in touch.

Charlotte Housego (9)
St John's CE (VA) Primary School, Ipswich

Summer

Summer's great cos of icy ice cream
Summer's great cos of icy ice cream and sandy sandcastles

Summer, summer, the best thing ever
Cos it's lovely and sunny, that's why I like it.

Summer's fab cos of pretty flowers with pretty petals
Summer's fab cos of pretty flowers with pretty petals and
The calming seas
Summer, summer, the best thing ever
Cos it's lovely and sunny, that's why I like it.

Summer's brilliant cos of spraying sun cream
Summer's brilliant cos of spraying sun cream and
The warm windy breeze

Summer, summer, the best thing ever
Cos it's lovely and sunny, that's why I like it.

Summer's great, fab and brilliant but
The worst thing about summer holidays
It's back to school in September.

Huda Abd (10)
St John's CE (VA) Primary School, Ipswich

The Big Lie

I am the fastest runner in my school and that's a big lie
I have been to the zoo a million times and that's a big lie
I have beat up a lion and that's a big lie
I am the best boxer in the world and that's a big lie
I got a Ferrari for my first car and that's a big lie
I am the best formula one driver and that's a big lie
I can divide 2 million by 9 million and that's a big lie
I can eat 100 burgers in one go and that's a big lie
I am the best footballer in my class and that's not a lie.

Joshua Moore (10)
St John's CE (VA) Primary School, Ipswich

Monsters!

There's a monster in my cupboard
Something blue not red
It lurks in the hallway
And even under my bed!

There's a monster in my cupboard
Terrifying it can seem
It followed me to school one day
Even into my dream!

There's a monster in my cupboard
It scares me in the rain
It scares me when the wind blows, but
My dad thinks it's in my brain!

I have a monster in my cupboard
It wears a tall black hat
It scares me in the morning
Then I worked out . . .

It was my cat!

Harriet Hughes (10)
St John's CE (VA) Primary School, Ipswich

The Sea

The sea can be blue
The sea can be green
The sea can be nice
Or the sea can be mean.

The sea can be soft
The sea can be rough
The sea can be rocky
Or the sea can be tough.

The sea can be salty
Or the sea can be naughty
But whatever it is
It's lovely to me
Because my favourite place
Is the deep blue sea.

Bethany Kenward (10)
St John's CE (VA) Primary School, Ipswich

I Love Food

I love fish
Which is served on a dish
I love cake
Which has just been baked
I love chips
Which are tasty on my lips
I love pies
Which are a feast for my eyes
I love peas
But they always end up on my knees
I love custard
But I hate mustard
But I really, really hate Marmite!

Thomas Floodgate (10)
St John's CE (VA) Primary School, Ipswich

Fun At The Seaside

Fun at the seaside
All day long
Eating ice cream
And playing ping-pong.

Building sandcastles
And splashing in the sea
Watching the ships sail past
With cargo for my tea.

Out on the jetty
Watching men catch fish
With my snorkel and flippers
In I go with a big *splish*.

Kezia Davey (10)
St John's CE (VA) Primary School, Ipswich

Forgotten

She stays there alone in a cold empty room
Helplessly waiting for her moment of doom
She hears a bang and her dad begins to shout
She wonders what she has done wrong
And what he is angry about
The tears flow like rivers down the soft cheeks of her face
She just wants all the pain to stop, to get away from this place
She starts to scream in the middle of the night
The neighbours hear but they turn out the light
The world around her begins to spin
As the freezing cold room around her starts closing in
So now she lies there, as cold as a stone
Living in a better place, a world of her own
Do not be sad for her as her life is at an end
For the bruises in her heart are beginning to mend
She no longer cries at night hoping for a better place
And the tears of pain no longer stream down her delicate face.

Abbie Jones (11)
St Mary Magdalene's RC Primary School, Bexhill-on-Sea

Cat Fights

Friendships are the bee's knees
They will come if you say please
Friendships are as hard as stone
They'll never break or groan
When all is said and done
Friendships are in everyone.

Fights emerge when people disagree
With every worthy he and she
Even if you're the best of buds
Fighting is not as clean as suds
Comments are a problem with girls
It gets them in tizzies and whirls
Breaking up is all a part
Of many girl's breaking hearts.

No one there to watch your back
Put onto the 'no mates' rack
Girls and boys pass you by
Other friends push in, ask why
Everyone goes to her
Oh how sad for that to have occurred
You are stubborn, you are sad
You are acting really bad.

Go up to her and say great things
Make her feel like she's on wings
All's forgiven, together again
You're stuck together like a lion and its mane
Across the playground you will go
Now both feeling not so low.

Ellie Stebbing (11)
St Mary Magdalene's RC Primary School, Bexhill-on-Sea

The Classroom

Peaceful, silent and lonely
The classroom waits
Waiting for the children
Their wonderful faces
He hears the clock ticking in the corner
Tick-tock, tick-tock.

Suddenly light fills him
The children are here
Laughter, chatter and singing he hears
His world is filled with joy
Not sorrow
All because he's got the children to follow.

The morning has come
The chatter has stopped
The teacher's voice
Booming like a boom box
The work is near
He waits to say goodbye
They wait to go
In a line as good as gold
But not for long
He waits for them
But not for long.

The end of school
The children go home
It's silent again
But he knows they'll be back tomorrow.

Jessie Sheppard (11)
St Mary Magdalene's RC Primary School, Bexhill-on-Sea

My Pencil

Slowly - with great care -
I am held softly in her hand
When she breathes I breathe with her.

Before I meet the paper, I am thrust into
The sharpener
But the pain only lasts a few seconds
Then I am tall, sparkling and new
What is this pain compared to love?

Finally! At long last!
I meet him
Waltzing and dancing at incredible speed
I prance with my Romeo
Then he leaves me and I am examined by my
Sweet mistress.

I enter the sharpener again
Oh what joy! What sweet bliss
My partner and I are joined again
Swaying and curling happily.

But what is this?
My mistress sighs
Maybe she too has a loved one.

No! No! No! No! No!
Before I am locked away again, I see a name at the top of the page
. . . It reads - *My Pencil!*

Lois Tucker (11)
St Mary Magdalene's RC Primary School, Bexhill-on-Sea

Wash, Wash, Good Enough For The Posh!

Left all alone to sleep in the darkness
Its eyes shatter, with the turned on lights brightness
The washing machine's mouth opens for laundry
As his owner, Dorothy, shoves it in.

Left alone once again
He thought he had a friend, but he was wrong
Now he'll sing a song.

Now he rumbles on, 'I would last longer with Calgon!'
He finishes the laundry
With no prize form Dorothy.

Now dead of the night
The washing machine's bored of the sight
He snores and grumbles
He's so full up he carries on and rumbles.

As he chimes, 'This is a boring time'
His mouth is closed
And his brain asleep
What will he dream in his
Midnight weep?

Cold with just a wooden door
And a bare kitchen floor
Now soon to rise
Thinking he's clever and wise.

Amelia Catherine Markfort (11)
St Mary Magdalene's RC Primary School, Bexhill-on-Sea

Pencil

My little pencil works hard all day
And the best thing is it does what I say.

Isaac Klugman (8)
St Mary Magdalene's RC Primary School, Bexhill-on-Sea

The Summer Sea

The sea is as blue as the summer
Sky and as green as the grass on
Land.

It has frothy fingers reaching to greet
The pebbles that lie lifelessly on
The scorching hot sand.

The shining sun beats down on the sea
Like a big drum
Causing the sea to ripple
Like a snake trailing through the
Long grass in the jungle.

As you watch the sea
It disappears
And makes you feel like you're
Floating in the breeze
High above with the sea birds that
Scream like children.

Like a ship sinking
The sun goes down
And the silver spoon moon
Rises to the top of the sky
And glistens on the sea.

Lauren Mary Louise Creasey (10)
St Mary Magdalene's RC Primary School, Bexhill-on-Sea

The Sea

The sea is a leaf floating in the breeze
It's as blue as the bright blue summer sky
The sea is calm and quiet
The sea is freezing cold when your skin meets it
The sand is like crumbling apple crumble
The sea is a peaceful and calm paradise.

Yasmin Davis (10)
St Mary Magdalene's RC Primary School, Bexhill-on-Sea

The Aeroplane

The aeroplane starts up its engine
His evil pair of eyes begin to appear
Rushing down the flight path
Taking off he begins to fly.

Up and up he goes
He lets his crimson wings free
Intending to be the main attraction
The battle is yet to begin!

He glides across the moonlit sky
Giving a wave to people below
His opponent is waiting
In a dusty fog
Waiting for the anger to spill out.

Approaching his opponent
There's a lump in his throat
They charge towards each other
With a mean grin on his face
Frightened in stern bravery
Bullets fire everywhere
The battle has ended, another one has begun!

Jessica Cumming-Bart (11)
St Mary Magdalene's RC Primary School, Bexhill-on-Sea

The Sky

The sky is a deep blue jellyfish
Floating around like a gorgeous blue
Forget-me-not when it flies in the
Stripy blue meadow.

Its fluffy petals climb the ladder to the heavens
When you look at the blue flowers your heart turns blue
And flies to your soul as you laugh to
The rhythm of the birds.

Miriam Calis (10)
St Mary Magdalene's RC Primary School, Bexhill-on-Sea

Howlets

One day I saw a baby elephant
He was small, cute and grey
He kept on walking backwards
We saw lots of animals that day.

We saw tigers, rhinos, lemurs and monkeys
When I saw them
They were really funky.

It was the first time I saw an elephant
So I had tears in my eyes
There was something flying around them
But I think it was flies.

We went in the play area
It was really fun
As soon as I got in the play area
Out came the sun.

At the end I saw the gorillas
They were white, black and grey
So now I would just like to say
Goodbye Howlets, see you again another day!

Mollie Docksey (9)
St Mary Magdalene's RC Primary School, Bexhill-on-Sea

Sunny Days

When it is a sunny day
I think it is May
When I go out in the sun
I have lots of fun.

I mess about and play around
Then I make a little sweet humming sound
I can explain the sun in so many ways
But these three are the best days.

Annabel Selvadurai (9)
St Mary Magdalene's RC Primary School, Bexhill-on-Sea

Dinosaurs

Big ones
Small ones
Slow ones
Fast ones

Dinosaur's fossils all around
Cute ones
Baby ones
Ugly ones
Spiky ones

Dinosaurs' tails
Strong tails
Soft tails
Fast tails
Slow tails

Dinosaurs' teeth
Dirty teeth
Clean teeth
Teeth covered in leaf juice
I love dinosaurs.

Mickey Cross (8)
St Mary Magdalene's RC Primary School, Bexhill-on-Sea

What Am I?

I wait patiently on the shelf
Waiting to be opened
I am filled with laughter
And sadness
Sometimes I fill your mind with
Hollowness
I am filled with lots of stories
And there I wait and wonder
Whose hand will grab me next?
What am I?

John Rey Ruiz (11)
St Mary Magdalene's RC Primary School, Bexhill-on-Sea

Poetry Explorers 2009 - The East & South East England

Egypt

Blazing sun beats down on the planet below
The sun god Ra is in a pleasant mood
He is pleased as his favourite slave has just made him fig wine.

His thoughts are powerful as a lightning bolt in the night sky
He can give people fears in the night just by a click of his fingers
He is powerful but he makes lots of people sad and angry.

He was not the only god in Egypt; there were lots of other gods
But Ra is special as he created the world
His tears created people, us wonderful people
He created other animals from dogs to camels.

One day he found he was just bored and had nothing to do
He created the sky god and all the other gods
To keep him company.

Once when he was dying, his people turned against him
He had to show them who was boss!
And he did!

Soon after his people turned against him he went
Into the afterlife . . .

Georgina May Pepper (11)
St Mary Magdalene's RC Primary School, Bexhill-on-Sea

Daniel

My mum's going to have a baby
A brand new giggling ball of fun
My mum's going to have a baby
A small, sweet, cute little baby
My mum's going to have a baby
Someone else to share my mum and dad with
My mum's had a baby
A baby boy my mum's had
My mum's had a baby
My new baby brother Daniel.

Chloe Leigh Fox (11)
St Mary Magdalene's RC Primary School, Bexhill-on-Sea

Bright Light

The room is filled with darkness
When I am off I'm heartless
If I am not used I become angry.

I wait for someone but no one is there
I wait for someone to care
But I wait and nobody is turning me on.

I feel presence in the air
Someone is coming to care
Someone is coming for me.

A person is going to turn me on
I'm being turned on, one, two, three
And then I shine the room with glee.

After a while they turn me off
And again I am angry
So I am out until the next day.

Hassan Takun (11)
St Mary Magdalene's RC Primary School, Bexhill-on-Sea

The Aeroplane

It runs up the long smooth runway getting ready to leap
Into the air
It's beginning its treacherous jump, it soars into the
Frosty daytime sky.

It glides elegantly through the ice cold air, slicing into the
Fluffy white clouds as it flies through
It stands tall in the air, higher than any building.

It flies towards its final destination, it sticks out its
Wheels preparing to land
It's landing, it bounces as it hits the rock hard ground.

It screams out as the brakes are suddenly slammed on
It glides to a halt, and rests till it is needed once more.

Niall MacDonald (11)
St Mary Magdalene's RC Primary School, Bexhill-on-Sea

The Rainbow Monster!

Ripples and splashes, colour flashes

The rainbow monster wants to play

Her whistle is whirling in the wind, calling
Her friends to play

The dolphin, the whale and the great sea snail all
Come to join her game

Bubbles bouncing, bubbles bursting, the
Smell of violets fills the air

The seagulls that fly high in the sky
Watch the fun below

Enjoy yourself happy ones because soon
It will be time to go.

Olivia Mackrell (11)
St Mary Magdalene's RC Primary School, Bexhill-on-Sea

Fireflame

Dazzles, amazes, bursts into flames
Wonders, angry, coloured hair flames
Blazing, *bang,* crash, whirling, shooting, indisputable, viciously
Furiously, fuming
Bang, she goes flying in her multicoloured ball gown
The coloured hair bursts into flames
Nobody had glimpsed her wonders before now
She dances from star to star, leaving a trail of sparks behind her
The fuming light of the Catherine Wheel zooms up behind her
The vicious flames shoot past the midnight feelings
Her amazing colours dazzle the crowds
Our hearts fill with passion, as the light goes away
As she shoots back down to Earth, she dies loudly, but
Sorrowfully.

Sophie Barret & Holly Wicks (10)
St Mary Magdalene's RC Primary School, Bexhill-on-Sea

Trees In Summer Breeze

The trees
Have a
Scent of
Breeze, it
Blows and
Flows and
The tree
Glows. The
Sky is
Blue, the
Clouds are
White and
Me of course
Is the same every time.

Alice Creasey (8)
St Mary Magdalene's RC Primary School, Bexhill-on-Sea

Until I Saw The Sea

Until I saw the sea
I did not know
That wind
Could wrinkle water so.

I never knew
That sun
Could splinter a
Whole sea of
Blue.

Nor
Did I know before
A sea breathes in and
Out upon a shore.

Ciaran Gaymer (10)
St Mary Magdalene's RC Primary School, Bexhill-on-Sea

I Miss You

I've missed you since you've been gone
I find it hard to go on
I've got a feeling inside
And it's making my heart cry, 'cause I'm missing you
And it's making me feel blue.
You made me believe that I could do almost anything
You stood right by me
Through the tears, through everything
You've been there for me, Dad, that's forever true.
You are the one that I'll always miss
Never thought I would feel like this . . .

Katie Wilson (11)
St Mary Magdalene's RC Primary School, Bexhill-on-Sea

The World's Most Feared Bully

The world's most feared bully brings down everyone in its path
roaring as loud as it can
Telling the world it is moving and ready to find another
                                            victim to attack.

The pace of this beast is tremendously fast
Dodging flaming fists of fury then it returns the favour
and regains the pride of being the fastest creature on the Earth
And the most destructive.

A true King of the sky, very strong and intelligent
It comes out for another day of destruction.

Andrew Creasy (10)
St Mary Magdalene's RC Primary School, Bexhill-on-Sea

The Star Gazer Lily

You stand tall and vivid
You let out your glorious fragrance
Showing off your dazzling skin
Gorgeous and delicate
While you sway in the wind.

Standing so elegantly
While you gaze at the sky
You look like a star compared to the rest
Everyone says you're royal
Which means you're the best.

Lauren Leigh Henson (11)
St Mary Magdalene's RC Primary School, Bexhill-on-Sea

Darkness

The street is full of darkness, my eyes fear the cold
There's a screaming from the silence
What is new seems old
The whisper from the pavement, the shutting from the door
My world is full of darkness, nothing more

The street is full of darkness, I listen for a friend
To help me through this ice age
And lead me to my end
The path I walk has ended; I collapse now on the floor
My world is full of darkness, nothing more.

Carys Rebecca Williams (10)
St Mary Magdalene's RC Primary School, Bexhill-on-Sea

The Tank

Tearing down the battlefield all cannons firing
Killing all the enemies in sight
Not stopping for anyone or anything
Leaving its mark till its job is done
There is no way to stop this monster from killing
All its prey
This almighty destroyer, this ferocious beast
Is the mighty one.

Jordan Billany (11)
St Mary Magdalene's RC Primary School, Bexhill-on-Sea

The Sun

The sun
Shines brightly
In the sky.
It is as warm as a fire
To keep us dry
But the best thing of all
Is that it's hot and
Warm.

Joe Lissamore (8)
St Mary Magdalene's RC Primary School, Bexhill-on-Sea

The Sea Is A Precious Sapphire

The sea is a precious sapphire
Its waves soft and calm
Like a palm tree dancing in the breeze
Frothy, giggling bubbles haul themselves up
Onto golden sand
The long hands of seaweed reaching up
The sea is a precious sapphire.

Olivia Murphy (10)
St Mary Magdalene's RC Primary School, Bexhill-on-Sea

My Talking Shoes

My talking shoes can talk
My talking shoes can lie
My talking shoes are black
My talking shoes are hard to walk in
My shoes are broken
My shoes are very, very small for me
What troublemakers they are!

Karina Barton-Monk (8)
St Mary Magdalene's RC Primary School, Bexhill-on-Sea

The Sea

The sea is a leaf floating in the gentle breeze
It's as blue as the bright blue summer sky
The sea is calm and quiet
The sea is freezing cold when your skin meets it
The sand is like crumbling apple crumble
The sea is a peaceful and calm paradise.

Olivia West (9)
St Mary Magdalene's RC Primary School, Bexhill-on-Sea

The Sea

The sea is like a singing lady floating
It's like a diamond just been polished
People swimming in the sea of fish
The skipping stones cross the river edge
Little kids making sandcastles
People say there's buried treasure.

Renie Vince (10)
St Mary Magdalene's RC Primary School, Bexhill-on-Sea

Flowers

They are green
They are red
They are blue
They are yellow too
Flowers are so beautiful
I've got one just for you!

Samuel Boreham (8)
St Mary Magdalene's RC Primary School, Bexhill-on-Sea

Roses

Roses sitting in my garden
Smelling beautiful in the summer
Sun
If anyone comes to pick my rose
They will find a prickle on their
Thumb.

Charlie Bonner (8)
St Mary Magdalene's RC Primary School, Bexhill-on-Sea

Being Eight Is . . .

Being eight is
Growing up a bit
Laughing like a shark with big teeth
Jumping on a bouncy trampoline
Climbing up a new light brown tree
Smiling like a slimy crocodile
Hopping like a one-legged ostrich
Running into a rainbow puddle
Fighting with my weird sister
Sprinting like the strong wind
Skipping like a mad kangaroo
Being eight is great!

Chiara Vidal (8)
Sacred Heart School, Wadhurst

Names

A is for Annie who plays with bouncy balls
B is for Ben who scribbles on walls
C is for Clara who loves dogs and cats
D is for Dan who wears funny hats
E is for Ella, she bought a furry coat
F is for Frank who looks like a goat
G is for Gemma she really likes cress
H is for Harry whose sister's name is Bess
I is for Izzy, always having a rest
J is for Jack in the red vest
K is for Katharine who's always in bed
L is for Luke, his favourite colour is red
M is for Mia who has a pet mouse
N is for Nick who's just moved house
O is for Olivia, her brother is funny
P is for Percy and he's got loads of money
Q is for Queenie, she has a sparkly ring
R is for Robert who often likes to sing
S is for Sally, she's scared of rats
T is for Tom, even more scared of SAT's!
U is for Una who's seen a prowling lion
V is for Vincent, his best friend is Brian
W is for Whillimena, she's committed a sin!
X is in Max, any race he will win
Y is for Yazmine who is very tall
Z is for Zax, is that a name at all?

Elizabeth Trippett (9)
Sacred Heart School, Wadhurst

Being Eight Is . . .

Walking into lamp posts
Yawning in the morning
Playing football outside
Scoring a goal
Playing for Chelsea
Sailing a pirate ship
Swimming with sharks in the sea
Meeting an alien from outer space
Eating thousands of sweets
Travelling to Antarctica
Thrashing someone at cricket
Being chased by a dinosaur
Getting out at night without your mum and dad knowing
Meeting the Queen at Buckingham Palace
Buying a car
Being at Wembley Stadium
Being eight is fantastic!

Oliver Taylor (8)
Sacred Heart School, Wadhurst

Being Eight Is . . .

Splashing the teachers,
Watching TV.
Squashing flies,
Buying toys.
Eating sweets,
Going to funfairs.
Staying up late,
Sleepovers - midnight feasts.
Parties (presents),
Being Indiana Jones.
Surfing,
Eating ice cream, chocolate, candy sticks and sweets
Parachuting off planes and blowing up the Temple of Doom.

Louis Griffiths (8)
Sacred Heart School, Wadhurst

Being Seven Is . . .

Being seven is . . .
Sometimes tiring
Ruining annoying brother's work
Swimming for miles
Pretending with your mad friends
Having silly sleepovers
And *parties of every kind*
Splashing in the pouring rain
Smiling like a sly fox
Sleeping for hours
Tidying your messy room
When you're feeling down
Your friends take away your frown
Shopping for hours
Just having fun!

Eleanor Knight (7)
Sacred Heart School, Wadhurst

Being Seven Is . . .

Not having baths
Not cleaning your bedroom
Playing football
Playing rugby
Not making your bed
Playing on the Playstation
Eating sweets
Not eating your vegetables
Being a Tom boy
Playing with your dogs
Meeting a dragon
Meeting a dinosaur
Getting tickled
Fighting with Olly
Having real good fun.

Rebecca Lond (7)
Sacred Heart School, Wadhurst

Being Seven Is . . .

Being seven is
Going on a high amazing roller coaster
Running like mad
Jumping really high
Running off hills
Hitting your sister
Watching horror movies
Playing football, scoring goals
Hopping for joy
Going really crazy
Crying like mad
Being seven is great!

Harry Thatcher (7)
Sacred Heart School, Wadhurst

Being Eight Is . . .

Bad! Doing all the chores.
Fun! Playing in the river.
Good! Playing with your brother.
Riding with your dad on his motorbike,
Climbing up trees,
Playing with your brother's toys,
Eating sweets.
Playing on your Nintendo DS,
Getting up before your mum says,
Having a water fight,
Playing on the trampoline,
Being 8 is great!

Theo Griffiths (8)
Sacred Heart School, Wadhurst

Being Eight Is . . .

Sometimes fun
Running out of danger
Playing football all the time
Sometimes dizzy
Winding up your brother
Seeing aliens
Falling out of a plane
Being late for Cubs
Learning French
Hard work
Really cool.

Ben Sanday (8)
Sacred Heart School, Wadhurst

Being Eight Is . . .

Growing up a bit
Believing in aliens
Flying in a UFO
Running away from my sister
Always playing games
Always having fun
Cool
Great
Awesome
Happy
Lovely.

Michael Ghose (8)
Sacred Heart School, Wadhurst

Being Eight Is . . .

Smiling like a sly fox
Swimming as fast as the wind blows
Being brave as a pirate
Laughing with your funny friends
Fighting with your big sisters
Being 8 is putting the blame on your sisters
Turning into a cheeky monkey
Being late for school
Being 8 is . . . *great!*

Eloise Langdon (8)
Sacred Heart School, Wadhurst

Pirates

If I were a pirate captain
I would boss my crew around
If I were a pirate captain
I would push my crew overboard
If I were pirate captain
I would drive the ship around
If I were a pirate captain
I would have a big hat
If I were a pirate captain
I would have a big sharp dagger
If I were a pirate captain
I would catch loads of fish
If I were a pirate captain
I would sail back home.

Rhys Brown (8)
South Wootton First School, Kings Lynn

The Chocolate Shop

I went in the chocolate shop
To get a chocolate bar
There were so many choices
I had to walk so far
I asked my mum what her favourite was
'Galaxy' she said,
'I'm not sure it's my favourite
I like Milky Way instead.'
So I asked my dad
And he said, 'Crunchie
Or . . . maybe I would prefer a Munchie!'
I just don't know what to choose
So maybe I'll just buy a new pair of shoes!

Megan Savage (8)
South Wootton First School, Kings Lynn

When I Am A Football Player

When I am a football player
I will crunch into tackles
When I am a football player
I will be captain
When I am a football player
I will never get substituted
When I am a football player
I will always score goals
When I am a football player
I will be very loyal
When I am a football player
I will listen to the crowd chant
But best of all I will lift trophies!

Adam White (8)
South Wootton First School, Kings Lynn

The Tiger And The Monkey

The tiger has sharp teeth
And he sneaks up on his prey
He likes to pounce in the jungle
He does this every day.

The monkey, he is cheeky
He eats bananas in the trees
He swings around from vine to vine
Moving through the leaves.

One day monkey met the tiger
The tiger looked and stared
The monkey threw banana peel
But the tiger went to bed.

Eden Daniell (8)
South Wootton First School, Kings Lynn

Chocolate

I love chocolate
Milk and dark
I even eat it in the park
I love chocolate
Nutty and crunchy
My favourite is a Munchie
I love chocolate
Day and night
Better take it out of my sight!

Aimée Colman (8)
South Wootton First School, Kings Lynn

Flowers

F lowers are pretty
L ovely and nice
O ver the gardens and pretty in vases
W allpaper has lots of pretty flowers on it
E very flower is pretty
R oses are pretty
S unflowers are nice.

Aimee Tivey (8)
South Wootton First School, Kings Lynn

What Should I Do With My Chocolate?

What should I do with my chocolate?
I just don't know
Should I melt it and put it on my ice cream?
Or should I turn it into sprinkles?
Should I turn it into a Kit-Kat?
I have no idea
Actually I think I should eat it as it is.

Sefton Henry Shillingford (8)
South Wootton First School, Kings Lynn

If I Won The Lottery

If I won the lottery . . .
I would get a golden horse
A sparkly house that will glow in the dark
A glittery cat that goes '*miaow, miaow*' in its sleep
A golden chicken that lays golden eggs.

Carla Sayer (8)
South Wootton First School, Kings Lynn

When I Watch The Sunset

When I watch the sunset at the beach . . .
I feel relaxed like Sleeping Beauty
I feel like I can touch the sun
I feel romantic
I feel like the day has come to an end.

Benita Bausbacher (8)
South Wootton First School, Kings Lynn

World War Two

W orld war two is scary
O verhead is black thick smoke
R un to the shelter, quick, quick
L ong ships were sunk by Germans
D one in 1939.

W orld War Two finished in 1945
A ir raid sirens screeching all around
R ationing food isn't nice.

T all aeroplanes are high
W orld wars are bad
O n an aeroplane are bombs.

Kirstie Windsor (9)
The Norman CE Primary School, Northwold

What The Bullet Sang

Suddenly, I accelerated
Through the air - the cold, grey misty air
But why do I hear screaming?
Now I turn to my love, he falls to the ground.
From the warmth of the gun to the coldness of his blood.

Harry Cater (8)
The Norman CE Primary School, Northwold

Hide In The War

B omb
O ver
M ost of England
B *omb!*

S *hhhhh!*
H ide
E verybody run
L ike mad
T o
E everybody's bomb shelter
R un, run, run and run.

Ella Wortley (8)
The Norman CE Primary School, Northwold

Pony Parade

P onies and horses can go to big shows
O n the horse box goes the show horse
N ow we're at the big show. The gun goes *bang!*
Y ou are in the lead! You jump the fences!

P ower is in your horse's body!
A chequered flag is waved. You cross the line!
R osettes are given out
A red rosette is handed to me. I won the race!
D rowned in sweat, I stumbled off my horse
E verybody is cheering for me!

Abigail Gostling (9)
The Norman CE Primary School, Northwold

World War 2 Acrostic Poem

W orld War 2
O h help us Lord
R eady to run
L ights out for the blackout
D ark as clouds going in.

W ar is evil
A silent city in the night
R un, run to the air raid shelter

2 people standing near a grave.

Alice Ireland (7)
The Norman CE Primary School, Northwold

I Remember . . .

I remember seeing the searchlights and evacuees
I remember shouting, 'Stop please!'
I remember my friend crying
I remember them dying.

I remember the planes overhead when
I was lying on my bed
I remember being filled with dread
I remember the Anderson Shelter
I remember the smell of my mum.

Olivia Rae (8)
The Norman CE Primary School, Northwold

The Bullet's Song

I was smiling as I zoomed through the sky
Looking down at the spooky, black, dusty ground
I heard banging aeroplanes and yelling
And then I reached my landing.

Hannah Bradford (8)
The Norman CE Primary School, Northwold

World War II

It shot like lightning really fast
The bullet went past me with a blast.

It went through my friend's bones
He fell to the ground on loads of stones.

The war was bad
Back to London with my mum and dad.

The air raid siren really loud
Back to London, glad and proud.

Euan Bradford (8)
The Norman CE Primary School, Northwold

WWII

I remember seeing huge flames and smoke appearing
I remember seeing bombs falling
I remember building an Anderson Shelter
I remember bombs falling like a helter skelter.

Amber Harris (10)
The Norman CE Primary School, Northwold

I Remember

I remember seeing bombs fly through the air
I remember seeing people waving goodbye
I remember seeing planes ready for flight
I remember seeing people ready to fight.

Kya Raven (9)
The Norman CE Primary School, Northwold

Magpie - Haiku

Black and white magpies
Bouncing through broken branches
Hunting for berries.

Hannah Muir (10)
The Norman CE Primary School, Northwold

Young Writers Information

We hope you have enjoyed reading this book - and that you will continue to enjoy it in the coming years.

If you like reading and writing poetry drop us a line, or give us a call, and we'll send you a free information pack.

Alternatively if you would like to order further copies of this book or any of our other titles, then please give us a call or log onto our website at www.youngwriters.co.uk.

Young Writers Information
Remus House
Coltsfoot Drive
Peterborough
PE2 9JX
(01733) 890066